BRAND

NEW
YOU

REINVENTING WORK, LIFE & SELF THROUGH THE POWER OF PERSONAL BRANDING

SIMON MIDDLETON

HAY HOUSE

Australia • Canada • Hong Kong • India
South Africa • United Kingdom • United States

First published and distributed in the United Kingdom by:
Hay House UK Ltd, 292B Kensal Rd, London W10 5BE.
Tel.: (44) 20 8962 1230; Fax: (44) 20 8962 1239.
www.hayhouse.co.uk

Published and distributed in the United States of America by:
Hay House, Inc., PO Box 5100, Carlsbad, CA 92018-5100.
Tel.: (1) 760 431 7695 or (800) 654 5126; Fax: (1) 760 431 6948 or (800) 650 5115.
www.hayhouse.com

Published and distributed in Australia by:
Hay House Australia Ltd, 18/36 Ralph St, Alexandria NSW 2015.
Tel.: (61) 2 9669 4299; Fax: (61) 2 9669 4144.
www.hayhouse.com.au

Published and distributed in the Republic of South Africa by:
Hay House SA (Pty), Ltd, PO Box 990, Witkoppen 2068.
Tel./Fax: (27) 11 467 8904.
www.hayhouse.co.za

Published and distributed in India by:
Hay House Publishers India, Muskaan Complex, Plot No.3, B-2,
Vasant Kunj, New Delhi – 110 070. Tel.: (91) 11 4176 1620; Fax: (91) 11 4176 1630.
www.hayhouse.co.in

Distributed in Canada by:
Raincoast, 9050 Shaughnessy St, Vancouver, BC V6P 6E5.
Tel.: (1) 604 323 7100; Fax: (1) 604 323 2600

A catalogue record for this book is available from the British Library.

ISBN 978-1-84850-496-7

Printed and bound by CPI Group (UK) Ltd., Croydon CR0 4YY

This book is for the dreamers
who may not feel brave or bold,
but who nevertheless know
the power of acting 'as if'.

CONTENTS

Introduction   ix

Chapter 1   What is a brand and why
             does it matter to you?   1

Chapter 2   The four building blocks of brand   15

Chapter 3   Your brand benchmark test   33

Chapter 4   Turning ambition and desire into
             personal brand strategy   61

Chapter 5   Establishing your brand values   71

Chapter 6   Putting your personal brand
             in context   83

Chapter 7   Who don't you want to appeal to?   95

Chapter 8   Using your imagination   105

Chapter 9   Brand 'positioning' and creating
             your unique place to stand   115

Chapter 10   Crafting your brand story:
             past, present and future   129

CONTENTS

Chapter 11	How to *tell* your brand story	141
Chapter 12	Bringing your personal brand to life visually	155
Chapter 13	Mustering your brand resources and using them effectively	167
Chapter 14	Hope, fear and the case for rational optimism	177
Chapter 15	Your 'customer experience': how to make it a good one	189
Chapter 16	What to do when your brand gets it wrong, which it will	203
Chapter 17	The end, the beginning, the permanent edge	217
	Acknowledgements	222

INTRODUCTION

This book is for the dreamers: the people who imagine a more exciting job, a more fulfilling relationship, a different way to spend their waking hours, doing something entirely new, fresh and thrilling with their lives.

Three vivid childhood memories prompted me to write this book and have contributed to my personal journey for the last three decades.

The first goes back to when I was eight or nine and a keen (actually, obsessive) reader of Hugh Lofting's Dr Dolittle books. Strangely, perhaps, it wasn't the push-me-pull-you or the other exotic creatures (not to mention the doctor's ability to talk to the animals) that fascinated me most about the books. Instead it was Dr Dolittle's entrepreneurial and action-oriented character. He seemed to be one of those people who just made things happen. He turned dreams into action. Even stranger is the fact that it was one of his more modest achievements that excited me the most.

In one adventure Dr Dolittle opened and ran a post office. It wasn't a great enterprise but it captured my imagination utterly. On long car journeys I would doze and daydream in the back seat of our Morris Minor, thinking through the process of opening and running a post office. This was an early stirring of desire for an enterprising life, although it took me a long time to get beyond daydreaming.

A few years later, when I was perhaps 14, there was a careers fair at school. Local companies talked to pupils about careers in engineering, accountancy, the armed forces and banking. By this time, I had given up my dream of opening a post office staffed by talking animals and was nurturing the notion of being a writer. Needless to say, the careers fair didn't have any literature about how to realize my dream. Instead, I found myself drawn into a long and miserable conversation with a man from Barclays, who thought I would be very well suited to train as a bank manager. I don't remember what I said to him but I do remember feeling that this was the moment at which my dreams would begin to die.

The third event happened about a year later. I got involved with a few kids in school who had formed a pretty ghastly pre-punk prog rock band that specialized in lyrical ballads about battles and witches. I was nominally the lyricist and the guitarist, and a very bad guitarist (and lyricist) I was, too. So bad in fact that, despite my powerful deep-rooted desire to perform, I did one performance and didn't touch a guitar or sing in public again for nearly 20 years. I decided, simply, that my dream of being a performer was about as achievable as that of running a business or being a writer.

So, at some point in my early teens I was ready to settle for what life dealt me. Not that it was intrinsically bad. I enjoyed a safe, comfortable, relatively affluent childhood. I was loved and cared for. But I was also aware that I was going to get stuck and that my dreams would remain dreams.

I have never believed that you can make things happen simply by dreaming: simply by being positive or by acting 'as if'. I do believe, however, that dreaming, being positive and acting are crucial elements in the endeavour of becoming the person that you want to be. And I absolutely don't believe that we have to settle for the outcome that life appears to have dealt us, or into which we have gently fallen.

It took me nearly 20 years to realize my dream of becoming a performer (I'm now a keynote speaker and a singer in a band). It took me 30 years to begin to fulfil my ambition of running a business (not a post office with talking animals, but a consultancy and my business Left Hand Bear). And it took me the best part of 40 years to become a professional writer.

Looking back, I think 20, 30, 40 years is too long to wait to fulfil your ambitions, so this book is all about fast-tracking those dreams. If I'd understood as a 14-year-old what I understand now, I wouldn't have had to wait so long. I'm determined that you won't have to do the same.

I know too many people for whom life in its many aspects, from work to relationships, seems to be something like a lobster pot. It's easy to travel in one direction but much harder, practically speaking, impossible, to travel in the other. In other words, for some people there is a sense of helplessness in the face of life's circumstances, which they manage by adopting a kind of stoic acceptance.

In one important philosophical and physical sense, this is true. Time moves in one direction. You can't undo the things you have done, nor un-experience your experiences, any more than you can un-stir the sugar from your coffee. To take this truth to mean that change is impossible, however, is to accept defeat when in fact we are not facing defeat but challenge.

This book then is about challenge: and specifically the challenge of changing your life from the one you have reluctantly accepted to the one that you dream about from time to time.

Perhaps you want to change your working life utterly, or simply improve your prospects at work. Perhaps you want to get a job, any job. Perhaps you face a conflict of some kind at work: a difficult boss or an impossible challenge. Perhaps you are facing redundancy. Maybe you have always wanted to start a business, or are struggling to launch one.

Or maybe the change you need to make is in your personal life: your relationships or self-image, or a desire to find personal fulfilment through a hobby or some form of creative endeavour.

The specifics of the change you require aren't important at this point. What *is* important is that you desire change. To move forwards, not in denial of what has come before, but nevertheless refusing to be defined or restricted by it. You are, after all, not a lobster in a pot but a human being with imagination, personality, abilities, energy and character.

This book is not one of those that promise if you follow certain behaviours you are guaranteed to achieve certain results. I can't make that promise. But it will show you how to utilize a particular set of strategies and techniques that I have used and seen working successfully in business: the art of branding, which has been my world for almost a decade.

But why, you might reasonably ask, should branding be of relevance and use in the task of changing my life? Well, there's a simple reason, which I will try to explain.

Branding is one of the key approaches, perhaps *the* key one, by which companies and other organizations, holiday destinations, cities and entire countries reinvent and shape their reputations in order to achieve success. Throughout the past century, and over the last 20 years in particular, branding has arguably become the single most important activity undertaken by any successful company, organization or place. Without the concept of brand and the art (and a bit of science) of branding, modern business simply wouldn't exist as we know it. If you think that I'm exaggerating, pause for a moment and consider the world's most successful businesses. What would Apple be without its 'brand'? Or Nike? Or Coca-Cola?

Now what is most interesting about branding, as far as we are concerned, is that businesses never see themselves as being stuck in the lobster pot. If a business doesn't like its circumstances, it endeavours to change. Businesses (and organizations and places) are rarely hampered by a sense that things can't be changed or improved. The simple reason for this is that businesses are not people: they don't feel or think or believe anything at all. They are not optimists or pessimists, introverts or extroverts. They are constructs. And because they are not hampered by the self-limiting beliefs of us humans, they can endeavour to become whatever their owners or senior management team want them to become by utilizing branding strategies and techniques. Sometimes these are used to make subtle changes to a company: to tweak its reputation, to explore new business opportunities or enhance performance in the market. Sometimes though, the same approaches are used to completely reinvent a business, or to utterly change the profile and standing of the entire business, or organization, or place. Businesses are not hampered by self-doubt, so they are free to create and re-create themselves to become what they wish to be (or at least to try).

These branding approaches can be applied just as effectively to our individual lives. In fact, I will go further and say that I have seen it happen. I have seen it work. I have seen lives change, all through the application of the techniques of branding.

And it's not in any way random or coincidental that these branding approaches can be applied usefully to us as individuals. We can use the ideas of brand and branding in our lives because the very power of branding as a business strategy stems from its origins in the human imagination. Branding is about telling compelling stories and the creation of 'meaning', which derives from our intrinsic human nature. We are meaning-makers and storytellers all. We have learned to apply the power of story to business, but I think many of us have forgotten how to apply it to our lives.

This book, therefore, is about taking a particular set of techniques (actually it might be better to look at it as a particular outlook or mindset), which derive from business, and applying them to your working life, creativity, relationships and, even, to your self-perception and inevitably your whole life. It is about learning to tell your story and creating your life meaning.

I should probably explain here that this book isn't about how to shake hands firmly and look people in the eye in interviews. Neither will it tell you how to complete a CV, about bragging or about how to gain a million followers on a social networking site.

We touch on some of those issues in passing but they are not the important ones. In fact, this book isn't about 'personal branding' in the conventional sense at all. There are books about 'personal branding' and plenty of people out there who will advise or coach you about your 'personal brand'. But by using this book, I hope you can achieve something more profound because it is written with the ambition of helping you to make real change in your life.

In fact, over the period of writing this book, I have come to describe the journey as one that is about finding and building 'character'. That old phrase 'character-building' seems to fit well. Another word that seems to describe the process is 'reinvention'.

What you are about to read is a kind of manual for building the character that you want for yourself; a guide to reinventing yourself as a character able to play an important, exciting and fulfilling role in the drama of life.

I said at the outset that this book is for the dreamers, but particularly those dreamers who have their feet on the ground while keeping their eyes on the future. I urge you not to stop dreaming, but rather to harness your dreams and make them real.

Throughout the book, you'll find the inspirational stories of just a few of the thousands of people who have used personal or business branding to successfully reinvent themselves and achieve their dreams.

The following chapters will give you an approach to doing what has worked for me, and others, and which I believe can work for you, too - regardless of your age, work history, qualifications or present circumstances.

Chapter 1

WHAT IS A BRAND AND WHY DOES IT MATTER TO YOU?

So, what possible relevance could the story of a 'brand' have to you and your life? Why would I want to tell you about famous (and not so famous) businesses, and why should you care? Well, the answer lies in being clear about the real definition of 'brand'.

Most people think – and it's easy to understand why – that a 'brand' is just another word for the 'logo' of a business. In other words, Nike has a very distinctive tick shape, known as 'the swoosh'. One of the curious things about the Nike brand, and this is indicative of an interesting aspect of branding in general, is that so many people know that that tick shape has been given a name. Why do so many of us know that Nike's logo is called 'the swoosh'? I think it is because there is a fundamental truth about brand; a brand is about stories and the logo having a name is a kind of story in its own right. And humans are hard-wired to love stories.

Regardless of whether we know the name of the Nike logo or not, that tick shape has become iconic. We see it everywhere: on shoes, on shirts and hoodies, in advertising campaigns and on packaging. We see it when we watch sports and on MTV. We see it in newspapers and magazines, on TV, at the cinema. Everywhere.

But is the swoosh Nike's brand?

No, it isn't. It's something else. The logo isn't the brand; it is just a trigger that reminds us of the existence of the Nike brand. Even more importantly, it is a stimulus which reminds us of the set of meanings that Nike wants to conjure up in our minds when we think about the brand. But it's not just about thinking, about what goes on in our heads, it's also about what we feel. The Nike logo, like any other, is designed to make us feel something: to trigger an emotional response.

There are actually three important things to remember here. First, that the logo is not the brand itself: the logo is one of the triggers designed to create a response to the brand. Second, that the response is just as much emotional (more so, actually) as rational. And third, that the logo is just one of the many tools that a brand can use to try to achieve the response it wants. We will look at all of those tools in due course.

So if the logo isn't the brand, what actually is a brand?

I have always defined brand as 'a set of meanings'. The brand of a product, or a company, or a place, or an individual is therefore the total of the meanings that it has in the minds and hearts of others. To put it another way, and let's say we're talking about a brand of coffee for example, the 'brand' is the sum total of all the things that people think and feel about that coffee.

In fact it goes even further than what you think or feel in a particular moment, because brand is influenced not only by what you have experienced yourself, but also by what you've heard from others, or what you've read in the papers or seen on TV. There are so many influences that it would be more accurate to describe the brand of our hypothetical coffee as being the sum total of everything that we think, feel, suspect, imagine, believe, hope, fear, have read or heard or seen about that coffee. The influences are so varied and so powerful, and the relationship between them so complex, that ultimately the 'brand' of the coffee doesn't really lie in the complete control of the coffee company at all (although the company would much prefer that it did), but in the collective heads and hearts of all the people who are exposed to it. In the end, it is the consumer who decides whether that brand of coffee is good, bad or indifferent, and therefore whether or not it will be a success in the marketplace.

But that can't be right, can it? Surely that logic would lead us to conclude that companies can't really do much about their brands after all. Well, no, far from it. In fact, companies have a huge opportunity to influence what people think and feel (and imagine and believe, and so on) about their products and thus to shape their brands. But they have to remember that brands are always about 'meaning' and, like beauty, meaning lies in the eyes of the beholder. So, brand owners are far from powerless, but they have to remember the sobering truth that the creation of brand meaning requires a pact between brand and audience – between 'them' and 'us'.

ABUNDANCE AND MISERY

So if brand is 'meaning', what does that actually 'mean' in practice and why does it matter? Why do companies, products, even places need to create 'meanings'?

The answer lies in a marketing concept known as 'the misery of choice'. This refers to the relatively modern phenomenon of abundance. In the developed world, even during times of hardship and recession, we live in times of abundance. All around us there are things and experiences to buy. I live in Norwich – it's only a small city, but if I was so inclined, I could eat out in a different pub or restaurant every night for around six months before having to visit any of them a second time.

And if you live in any of the world's capitals, you could eat out forever, choosing a different restaurant every night because by the time you got back to the first one again, it would, in all probability, have been taken over and reopened under a different name, serving completely different food.

If you want to buy a car you are presented with a choice of at least a couple of dozen makes and models, even if you narrow it down to a class of car such as a small family hatchback.

When you need to replace your laptop computer, how do you choose from the staggering array of makes and models? And if you want to select a new mobile phone contract, how do you unpick all the benefits of the plethora of different tariffs available?

This 'abundance' of choice applies even if you want to buy something as simple as a magazine or a newspaper, a washing-up liquid or toothpaste.

This is the misery of choice, and faced with an intimidating array of options we have come to use a system of signs and associated meanings to navigate our way quickly and effectively. That system is what we refer to as branding.

We buy a certain type of toothpaste each time because we have come to feel comfortable with that particular brand. And why do we feel comfortable? It is because we have come to associate that toothpaste with certain meanings. It tastes and feels fresh, perhaps. Or we have come to trust that it protects our sensitive teeth from pain when brushing. Or we are comfortable that it doesn't contain unnecessary chemical agents, so we think it is safer for our children. Or it has a mild whitening effect. Whatever the reason, the point is that we don't have to think through this set of meanings every time we purchase. We select the brand we know because it is the shortcut to the meanings that are our guide through the misery of choice.

Toothpaste is an odd example, you might be thinking, because toothpaste isn't really something we dwell on too much. And actually, I can almost hear you say, sometimes we simply buy the toothpaste that is 'on offer' in some way.

Yes, that's all true. In fact, toothpaste falls into the category of what marketers call 'low-involvement purchases', which means precisely that – we don't get too involved in the whole thing (either emotionally or intellectually). Yes, we are influenced by special offers, but we have a very strong tendency (even with low-involvement products) to revert to our preferred brand, or even our preferred kind of brand. So we might well choose the special offer product that we have never heard of, but we are much more inclined to do so if the special offer product appears to have some equivalence to our usual brand. In other words, we like offers but we still look for meaning.

It's for this reason that there is so much brand imitation in supermarkets. Breads, cereals, biscuits, toothpastes and many other consumables will tend to look a lot like each other, and particularly like the established and trusted market leader: they are all trying to take some reflected positive meaning for themselves. Being cheap rarely wins in the battle for consumer loyalty by itself.

BRAND CHOICES AND WHAT THEY MEAN

So, if even low-involvement purchases utilize brand meaning, when it comes to high-involvement purchases, such as a new car, brand meaning is extraordinarily powerful.

Let's think about cars for a moment. BMW means something quite different from Volvo does it not? Even if you are not remotely interested in cars, you will have heard the word 'safety' associated with Volvo.

The two Swedes who founded Volvo in 1919 were acutely aware that motoring, particularly at that time, was a rather dangerous activity. Cars didn't have any of the safety features of modern vehicles, roads were unregulated and drivers untrained. So these two progressive thinkers set out to create a car that was safer than others. Safety is not an affectation of Volvo's marketing people: safety is a meaning that is built into the fabric of the company. Volvo, in a very real sense, means safety.

BMW, on the other hand, means something quite different and it is usually associated with the driver's experience. The rear-wheel drive and engineering makes BMWs (if you like driving) great fun to drive. They are powerful, precise, stable and so on. So driver experience has become the meaning of BMW. For many years the company used the slogan 'The ultimate driving machine' to express this thought. In recent years they have changed to the simple one-word slogan 'Joy'. It is trying to express the same idea, but with a softer and less masculine feel.

Whether you or I like cars, these particular brands or their slogans, is not the point. The point is that successful brands (sometimes quickly and sometimes over decades) establish a small set of meanings that are resonant with enough people to give them a clear 'position' in the terrifyingly muddled marketplace.

So if your prime interest is safety, then Volvo will be on your list of cars to consider. If you are interested in the excitement of driving, then a BMW will have more appeal, and so on.

Coca-Cola is 'real', meaning original, and by implication better than any other fizzy soft drink. New Zealand is 'pure' and 'different', meaning unlike any other holiday destination in the world. John Lewis offers 'quality, service and value'. The BBC is 'trusted'. Rice Krispies are 'fun'. McDonald's is consistently 'satisfying' wherever you go.

I could go on at great length. Some brands have a meaning that can be expressed in one simple word – such as Volvo – to a degree where they virtually own the concept. Others are more layered or nuanced.

The common thread of great brands is that they tend to have either one single, powerful meaning above all others, or a small, closely linked set of complementary meanings

A MEANINGFUL LIFE

It is worth dwelling on this concept because I want you to think about your meaning or set of meanings and how they might help you to achieve your ambitions in work and in life.

Let's keep those two (work and life) separate just for a moment or two longer and let me give you a personal example that lies at the heart of why I have written this book.

I was a latecomer to the idea of creating 'meaning' for myself. I searched for it for three decades but I didn't really understand what I was looking for. The big mistake I made repeatedly was in thinking that meaning lay outside of how I spent my working days and, until a few years ago, I was somewhat divided from myself.

I had, if you remember, a childhood fantasy of running a post office or shop. Later I dreamed of becoming a writer. Like many teenagers, I fantasized, too, about being a singer, a pop star! I also obsessed for several years about Grand Prix motor racing, and in the early 1970s I applied for a mechanic's apprenticeship with the British Formula 1 motor-racing team BRM. I managed to get an interview with the chief mechanic, who was astute and experienced enough to realize that I wasn't really interested in becoming a mechanic at all, but was in fact set on becoming a driver. I had read the story of how the great Graham Hill had got his first break that way. The chief mechanic knew that story, too, and I was sent away heartbroken.

None of this muddled struggling with ambition is in any way unusual. And I went on with my muddled struggling for a long time to come. I thought I had talent in writing and art and planned to study art history at university. But I did spectacularly badly in my A-levels and ended up taking a degree in education, combined with a primary school teaching qualification, although I never wanted to teach. On graduating I tried to get into the local newspaper on their graduate journalism-training scheme, but the scheme closed the year I needed it. Instead, I got a junior job in a PR consultancy. For the best part of five years I learned to write, some of the rudiments of marketing and I grew up a little. But I still failed to integrate my work with 'me'. I was, in a very real way, alienated from myself.

I thought that all the 'meaning' in my life lay outside my work. I married at 19, while still at college (and am still married, very happily, to the same person, 33 years later), and our first child, Paul, was born when I was 24. At home I wrote endless (rather bad) poems and short stories: a few even got published. But my two worlds of work and life were separate. My 'meaning' lay in my marriage, my family and my writing, while I spent long working days engaged in something quite separate: something that held no meaning for me at all.

It took me many years to integrate my working life with my 'life', and it was only when I managed to merge the two that I transformed from being frustrated to fulfilled.

And the process by which I made that transformation might well be referred to as the creation of meaning. Some people would call it reinvention. What I have learned in recent years, by being involved in the worlds of business and branding, is that I actually re-branded myself. Or to be more accurate, I created a brand for myself for the first time.

And I don't mean that I dressed myself up superficially to be something different. I mean that I deliberately turned myself into a 'project'. I gave myself a new set of meanings, which successfully integrated my work with the rest of my life.

In so doing, I transformed my life inside and out. I became happier and healthier, and more at ease in the world.

I didn't make my transformation until I was a little over 50 years old. You don't have to wait that long. It's not a question of age or experience but of strategy.

Now it is time for the first of many exercises that you'll find throughout this book. First, find a notebook, or create a new file on your computer and title it appropriately, perhaps 'Brand Me', to record your answers and findings, and refer to as you journey through your transformation.

None of the exercises are complex but they are meant to be challenging. Rather than quiz-type exercises with pre-determined answers, you simply respond to open questions. There are no right or wrong answers and in all likelihood you will be the only person ever to read what you write. Write a little or write a lot, use sentences or just scribble phrases: it is up to you. The important thing is to try to focus your thinking, and completing the exercises can be a useful way to do that. You might even think of them as a kind of meditation.

EXERCISE I: YOUR MEANING NOW

First, recall what you've read in the previous pages about brand 'meaning'. Remember that brands are about the creation of sets of meanings. Creating your personal brand is about the creation of meaning, too.

This exercise is very simple, but it requires you to be honest (really honest) in order for it to have value. We will revisit it later, at which time some of your answers may change.

For now, write down the 'meanings' that you think you represent in the minds and hearts of those who know you – how do others perceive you and your values? I have suggested a number of headings below, which you might like to use because it may be that your meanings might vary depending on your audience.

Partner

If you have a life partner, make a note about what he or she thinks or feels about you. It might be that they think of you as 'kind' or 'energetic', or 'sporty' or 'lazy'. Keep going until you've really captured what they think and feel about you. Remember to be completely honest with yourself.

Family

Include your children, your parents, your siblings and other relatives under this heading. You may want to separate them out.

Friends

Include those closest to you, as well as more casual acquaintances.

Colleagues

Try to include the colleagues with whom you have less than positive relationships, as well as your actual work friends.

Your boss

Most of us have more than one boss, but you can choose the most appropriate one, or two.

Yourself

Try to step outside yourself and be as objective as possible here. What are your meanings to yourself?

That exercise might have been quite painful, but don't worry, this is a journey that you're on now. You are now your own brand project and you're already making progress.

REAL-LIFE REINVENTORS ❢
Dr Izzeldin Abuelaish: medical doctor and peace campaigner

In 2009, Israeli shells fell on Dr Abuelaish's family home in Gaza, killing three of his young daughters and their cousin. Overwhelmed by grief and despair, and having nowhere else to turn for help, the doctor phoned an Israeli journalist friend. As a result, the horror was transmitted live on Israeli television and later to the wider world through YouTube. Rather than grow embittered about his loss, Dr Abuelaish determined that the girls' deaths should not be in vain and turned his personal story of tragedy into a powerful peace campaign. His mission is to show the world, through this tragic story, that not every Palestinian is motivated by revenge. Dr Abuelaish is now a professor of global health at the University of Toronto and has travelled the world campaigning for peace. He has won humanitarian awards, been nominated for the Nobel peace prize and has established a charitable foundation, Daughters for Life, to support the education of girls.

Chapter 2

THE FOUR BUILDING
BLOCKS OF BRAND

We've thought about the meanings that brand creates for companies and products, and we have acknowledged that those meanings are not entirely in the control of the owner of the brand, or in your brand's case, You.

There is a sense in which brands can be said not to exist at all, except as a kind of collusion or pact between the brand and the audience.

Volvo is synonymous with safety only until the car-buying public around the world decides that another brand has stolen the 'safety' crown. You may remember the extraordinary furore caused by Coca-Cola in the early 1990s when it introduced 'New Coke', which offered a new formulation and a subtly different flavour. Coke fans were outraged and the company was terribly damaged. Coca-Cola's crime wasn't the introduction of a new variant, as the company has done this very successfully many times since, but the implicit repositioning of its key product. To make way for New

Coke, the original flavour was to be discontinued. Coke drinkers interpreted this as a deep and unacceptable betrayal. If their much-loved product – which had such a powerful connection to their culture and lives – was being replaced, they felt that they were less important as customers, as people. The New Coke debacle wasn't about flavour. It was about the company failing to remember that the reputation of its brand lay with its audience. Coca-Cola was seen as breaking a profound pact with its customers. Forgiveness was a long time coming and the story is still a black mark against the Coke brand to this day.

So, brands are about pacts, but how do you create such a pact? By obeying four vital principles: principles that will be referred to again and again in this book and which I hope will form the solid pillars upon which your personal brand will be built.

Over the years I have worked with many brands, and have observed many more: brands of every size and kind, in every type of market, in the UK and beyond. No matter how diverse, the successful brands have four key factors in common. They express them in different ways, and with different emphasis, but the same four factors always seem to be present nevertheless. And it is these four elements that I believe determine the brands' success in creating 'meaning' and thus effectively forming the vital pact with their audiences.

The four key factors are:

- Being authentic
- Being highly distinctive

- Being compelling

- Being excellent

Let's look at each of these in turn and, as we do, start to think about how each of them applies to you. Yes, that's right, 'You', reading this, right now. These four factors are not only the building blocks of great brands, they will also become the foundations on which the changes you wish to make in your life will be built.

BEING AUTHENTIC

Great brands are authentic, which is to say they are true to themselves and they don't make claims about themselves that aren't based on reality. Furthermore, although great brands tell stories, and create mystery and drama about themselves, they have a strong tendency NOT to tell lies. There are two key reasons for this. One is that lies have a tendency to be found out and the other is that lies are simply unnecessary for great brands and get in the way of effective storytelling.

Think about Apple for a moment. Whether or not you're an Apple fan – and I should declare my position here and say that I am – you will acknowledge that Apple has become one of the world's most successful and most admired brands.

There are many interesting things to note about Apple's brand, but for now let's just think about the phenomenon of authenticity. Apple is dramatic in its product launches and in its legendary store openings.

Apple tells stories about its products, its organization and its people but it has never, to my knowledge, felt the need to be inauthentic. This isn't just a matter of not telling lies (the minimum we expect from successful business is 'honesty'). Authenticity includes straightforward honesty, but it is a bigger concept than that; it really refers to an idea about being true to oneself. Apple, in other words, has been consistently true to itself and its meanings.

What Apple 'means' to most people is a combination of ever-advancing technology and a certain elegance of design and function. In return, Apple products are pleasing to the eye and to the touch, as well as being simple and generally intuitive in the way they work. If Apple suddenly (or even gradually) began to produce products that weren't designed with the same elegant aesthetic and ease of use, then we would start to feel that Apple was no longer being 'authentic'. Apple fans may not all use that word specifically, but they would share the nagging feeling that Apple had somehow broken its pact with them and that it was no longer being true to its promise.

To stay with Apple for a moment, its co-founder and head honcho, the late Steve Jobs, was famous for making his keynote presentations dressed in what became a 'trademark' style: training shoes, jeans with no belt and a tucked in black roll-neck sweater. His cropped hair and stubbly beard was the look of the middle-aged computer geek meets off-duty college professor. The outfit was the same every time for years, but that doesn't make it inauthentic. On the contrary, it actually conveyed part of the authentic meaning of the Apple brand. Steve Jobs carried the Apple brand message in wearing what he wore. His clothes were casual and relaxed because using an Apple device is easy and accessible. And restrained, because the wow factor is in the design of the products. His clothes were consistent in every respect because he wanted us, on the one hand, to understand that nothing had changed, it's business as usual: Apple are doing their usual thing of announcing yet another brilliant product development. And on the other hand, he wanted us to look at the product, not at him.

The same can be said about Apple's advertising. Apple's TV commercials are markedly less 'creative' than a great deal of other advertising. They don't use gimmicks or drama to promote the products. They simply present them and describe their advantages. In fact most Apple ads present just one advantage. With the launch of the MacBook Air, for example, all the focus was on just one point of difference from the competition: remarkable thinness. The importance of thinness lies not in any real practical advantage to the consumer, but in its authenticity to the Apple brand. We have come to expect Apple products to move the goalposts of design with each new launch. It is part of the authentic promise of the brand. The thinness of the MacBook Air was an expression of Apple's loyalty to that promise.

Virtually everything that Apple does is considered, which is to say it is thought about and weighed up against the company's understanding of its own brand. But being considered (thinking about things) does not equate to a lack of authenticity. Now if

Apple launch a product with the presenter dressed as a circus ringmaster, that will be inauthentic and we will be justifiably concerned that something is amiss. Or if – and this is equally unlikely – Apple feels the need to hide a product's limitations with a big hollow fanfare of exaggerated claims, or by trying to distract our attention with 'clever' advertising, then we will be rightly suspicious.

WHY DOES IT MATTER FOR YOU?

Authenticity matters to you because it matters to your 'audiences'. Whatever you do, wherever you go – even when you are completely alone – you have an audience. Your audience might be a potential business partner, an employer or your boss, someone you're trying to make friends with, or to flirt with. Your audience might even be your own sense of self (your conscience, as some people would call it). At the other extreme, if you are a performer of some kind, or a high-profile personality, your audience might number in the thousands or millions.

But no matter how diverse in size and kind, audiences have one thing in common: they are fantastically good at sensing inauthenticity. They won't always be conscious of it, of course, and people can be temporarily duped or charmed, but sooner or later inauthenticity will be detected, and the result is always disappointing for all parties.

We've all met people who brag, and encountered situations where we're not quite sure whether to believe someone or not. Sometimes, we can't quite put our finger on what it is about a person or their claims that doesn't quite ring true, or feel right. Some people call it a 'bullshit detector'. We've all got one, although it's true that some of us have learned to use it better than others.

The bullshit detector is listening out for a lack of authenticity. So important is authenticity to us that we are inclined to prefer dealing with unpleasant people who seem to us as if they're telling the truth than with very engaging, entertaining and charming people who we feel are not being quite candid with us.

We've all said, or heard said, something like: 'I do like him, but I wouldn't trust him as far as I could throw him', or 'Oh, she's great fun, but you have to take her with a pinch of salt'.

In building your personal brand, I don't want you to focus on being 'likable' or 'great fun' but rather on being authentic: true to yourself. This is a founding principle of branding and, I believe, a key principle of creating the character that you want to become. Along the way, though, you will also discover that there are limitations to being 'true to yourself' and that you also have to be true to your audiences. We will return to authenticity presently, with an exercise, but first, let's look at the other three pillars.

BEING HIGHLY DISTINCTIVE

Marty Neumeier, one of my favourite writers about brands, says that brands have to be first and foremost 'different... no really different'.

I agree absolutely with Neumeier that no truly great brand has ever been created by imitating another brand. It's a vital concept, and another of the four essential pillars of branding.

For example, one of my favourite brands of all time is Volkswagen and it's a good reminder of the importance of being 'different'. Go back to the 1950s and 1960s when Volkswagen was building its brand in the USA and picture the archetypal American car of the post-war decades. Big. Wide. Long. Covered in chrome. Lights mounted on tail fins, which echoed the designs of Cold War jet fighters, the 'space race' and sci-fi comics. American cars of this period were about swagger and glamour and suburban aspirations.

Volkswagen faced a problem. Their humble little 'Beetle' had to overcome a number of challenges. First, it was German, and, specifically, it had originally been a product of a regime that had caused the world's greatest ever conflict. And, as if that wasn't enough of a barrier, the car was (by American standards at least) tiny, impractical, underpowered and ugly. Even the brand name was wrong. VW! The people's car! The Americans didn't want a 'people's car'. They wanted aspirational cars. Cars fit for the American dream. You could have argued that everything about the VW was wrong.

And yet, little by little, year on year, by rigorously holding onto its distinctiveness (and, lest we forget, its authenticity) the VW came to be loved and admired across the USA. Not by everyone – the VW Beetle has never been the country's bestselling car, even in its class – but by people who, for one reason or another, were drawn to its extreme distinctiveness. The Beetle didn't look like any other car, or sound like any other car, or feel like any other car and, extremely importantly, the VW was not a 'concept' car. It wasn't 'wacky' or 'crazy'. It still, after all, functioned like a car. It still carried a family plus luggage, and steered like any other car while being completely and utterly distinctive. Round where other cars were angular. Short where others were long. Modest, where others were showy. Engine at the back! Air-cooled. And so on.

The point is that the original VW wasn't just a little bit different from its competitors, it was utterly and completely different. So different in fact that its fundamental shape and concept lasted, with only gradual modifications, for some five decades. It's hard to think of many cars that have achieved the same longevity of brand difference.

And what does that mean for you: for 'brand you'? Am I encouraging you to go out of your way to shock or surprise your audiences by looking or behaving weirdly, or being wacky? No, I am not. I'll repeat that to make sure: I'm not encouraging you to be weird, wacky, crazy or whatever other word you want to substitute. I don't want you to be the office clown.

What I do want you to do though is to think about the characteristics that positively and definitely make you distinct from everyone else. The VW bug didn't actually set out to be different from its post-war American competitors. It was designed in different circumstances entirely. What it then did with huge success was to celebrate and explain those differences: it never apologized for being different. Instead, it told great stories about those differences. And there'll be an exercise coming along soon in which you can think about and start to record the things that make you different.

BEING COMPELLING

I use the word compelling because I like its strength. It sounds determinedly purposeful. Some people may think the idea of being 'compelling' speaks too much of trying to force others to do your will, but that's not what I mean by it. Another word you might prefer is 'inspiring' (though my problem with inspiring is that it's overused and its meaning has been diluted). Either way, being compelling or inspiring is one of the characteristics of great brands and I want it to be one of your characteristics, too.

Great brands are compelling in the sense that they 'do' something or 'are' something that commands our attention. Great brands behave in ways that intrigue, or excite, or move their audiences.

Now it's important to make clear that this quality of being compelling doesn't demand, or even necessarily imply, that great brands always behave dramatically.

Take the example of the department store John Lewis. There's nothing at all dramatic about it. It's a quiet, unsurprising brand. Whichever John Lewis store you enter, you can be pretty confident, nay certain, about what you'll find. John Lewis doesn't really change very much. It stays up to date. It stays smart. No one, however, would claim that it's at the cutting edge of style or retail experience. But therein lies its quality of being utterly compelling. For a certain kind of British consumer, John Lewis provides unrivalled reliability. Every store looks and feels the same (pretty much) and has the same range of goods (pretty much). The decor is smart, but unexciting. The layout is clear, but hardly stimulating. The service is friendly and unfailingly helpful, but undemonstrative. In many ways, John Lewis provides the epitome of what its loyal customers hope a department store will provide.

It provides quality products, way above average service and (though no one shops in John Lewis because they think it is cheap) it provides a value promise that has become world famous: 'Never Knowingly Undersold'.

Ironically, it is the accumulation of all this modesty that makes John Lewis such a compelling proposition. We are, in a sense, compelled to respect it because, year after year, it fulfils its simple, but far from easy, promises.

By way of dramatic contrast, think about a US president, specifically Barack Obama. For anyone outside the USA, American elections have not been thrilling affairs in recent decades. But Obama's first election campaign was something different.

What made Obama's road to the White House so exciting, so compelling? Well, of course, there was the obvious factor of the possibility of the first black president. In itself that was a compelling, historic promise. But there was more to Obama's campaign than race. Far more. Obama presented a number of qualities, or stories if you will, that made him not only stand out from the rest of the candidates of recent years, but placed him in a class all of his own.

For one thing he was a published writer: an author of serious books about serious ideas. For another, he was clearly a man not just of energy and youth, but also of integrity. Then there is his charisma. Many politicians are charismatic, but Obama is charismatic in a way that is not simply about charm and an ability to work a crowd or deliver a speech, but in a way that seems to make a genuine and powerful emotional connection with people. Obama never looks like he is trying to charm: only to connect.

Finally, and by no means the least in this list, Obama presented a simple but hugely powerful and emotionally resonant idea: hope. Captured in the memorable campaign line 'Yes, we can', Obama's campaign promised hope for change for millions of Americans like no one else's since John F. Kennedy.

At the time, Obama's election campaign inspired people's emotions, their intellects and their imaginations, and ultimately, of course, their actions – they joined the campaign and voted for him. Not a bad model to have in mind when you begin to think about your personal brand.

BEING EXCELLENT

Excellence used to be a big idea in business. The management guru-of-gurus Tom Peters co-authored a hugely influential book called *In Search Of Excellence* in the early 1980s. Japanese management theory and practice worked towards excellence in constant small steps of continuous improvement. Among the many management slogans concerning excellence was the stimulating idea that 'good is the enemy of great'. In other words, according to adherents of this outlook, it was wrong to be satisfied with 'good enough' and important to strive constantly for a kind of corporate perfection.

In management theory and practice in the 21st century, however, the notion of excellence has somewhat fallen from grace. We live in a faster world now, a world where brands rise and fall swiftly and dramatically. A world in which, as soon as a brand has risen to dizzy heights of achievement – think of Facebook and its extraordinary rise in just a few years – it is already vulnerable to attack and predictions of its demise. An era in which some of the biggest and highest-profile businesses in the world, from oil companies to banks, seem to be based not on the pursuit of excellence, but profit above all else.

So, excellence isn't the buzzword it once was, but, ironically perhaps, I think that increases its significance and power as a marker of great brands. Apple, of course (yeah, I know), is a brand that typifies excellence in action. Apple wouldn't have achieved such greatness if it was simply an idea: it actually had to deliver on its promise of accessible and beguiling uses of technology. When Apple stops delivering that excellence of experience, its days will be numbered.

Amazon didn't become the world's greatest online retail brand just by being quite good, but by delivering (most of the time, for most customers) an excellent experience and result. Google is the greatest of the search engine businesses because for most people, most of the time, it delivers an excellent experience and excellent results.

In a way, it all depends on your definition of the word 'excellent'. My trusty Chambers dictionary says that excellent means 'surpassing others in some good quality', and 'good in a high degree'. Note that it doesn't say anything about perfection, and that's terribly important.

Like great commercial brands, as you develop your own brand you will need to surpass others 'in some good quality' and be 'good in a high degree'. You don't, however, need to be, or even to strive, to become perfect.

This book, like business and like life, is not about the achievement of perfection. Instead, it is about being good in a high degree and about surpassing others in some good quality.

EXERCISE 2: YOUR FOUR PILLARS

As in the previous exercise, and the rest that follow, remember that there are no right or wrong answers: just honest or less-honest ones. The more honest you are, the further you will be taking yourself along the journey.

Being authentic

Create two columns, one marked 'Authentic' and the other 'Inauthentic'. Now think about as many aspects of your life as you can (work, personal life, everything) and note whether they should be in the Authentic or the Inauthentic column.

How do you decide? Trust your instincts. One way to approach this exercise is to think whether any given aspect of your life really 'feels like me'. It's not just a matter of whether you enjoy something or not – it's more a matter of whether you are being yourself (being true to yourself) in this aspect.

Being highly distinctive

This is a simple concept but a bit more challenging in the doing. I'm not asking you to think of things about you that are unique. We're not looking for unique, just distinctive. Make a list of the things that give you your individuality, which make you interesting and set you apart from other people.

For example, if I were making the list about me I would include that I am left-handed, not a bad singer (though very bad at finding harmonies), a moderately competent acoustic guitarist, a good conference speaker, a published author, very comfortable performing in front of large audiences.

Now it's your turn... don't hold back.

Being compelling

This is about noting the reason, or reasons, why people find you engaging: the qualities, or skills, or behaviours that you are most noted for. This might be challenging for you right now but take a stab at it. Are you, for example (as my wife Sheila is), noted for extraordinary support to your friends and family? Or are you known as the best person to organize a party or other event? Or maybe you're an exceptional listener, a brilliant gardener or the best joke-teller. Or are you simply fearless? It doesn't matter what it is: it just matters that you acknowledge and note it.

I believe everyone has something compelling about him or her: something potentially irresistible to others. If you can uncover it then it could become a key element of your brand.

Being excellent

Please remember that we're not after perfection: just being very good at something, or working towards being good at something. When I first joined a band I was a rotten singer and a truly terrible guitar player. That was 20 years ago. I'm better now but I'm nowhere near excellent, although I strive towards it every Saturday morning at rehearsal and at every gig, no matter how small.

What do you have the potential for excellence in? This is so wide open that I won't give examples. But there is something (there always is): you have a talent, or a gift, or you've worked hard to achieve competence in something. Write it down and don't be falsely modest.

REAL-LIFE REINVENTORS ❢
Leo Babauta: leading blogger and expert on simple living

When San Francisco-based Leo Babauta, 'a regular guy, father of six kids, husband and writer', successfully quit smoking in 2005, it set off a chain reaction of other powerful changes. 'I had tried and failed to quit smoking before, and when I was successful this time, I analysed it and learned from it and was inspired by my success,' he says. Next came several marathons, losing weight – which he'd failed to shift for years – eating healthier food, paring down to a minimalist lifestyle and becoming organized. Along the way Leo wrote his story on his 'zenhabits' website, and was named by *Time* magazine as one of the top 25 blogs in the world, with 200,000 subscribers tracking his progress and asking for advice and information. His life is simple, frugal and clutter-free and others want to live the same way. Now Leo's story has become his business and he has also written a bestselling e-book, *The Power of Less*.

Chapter 3

YOUR BRAND
BENCHMARK TEST

Now it is time to get down to the quintessence of whether your current 'personal brand' is working for you, or whether you have a 'personal brand' at all yet.

I want to reiterate that the concept of brand can work for you regardless of your current circumstances. You may be unemployed or a high-flying executive. You may own a highly successful (or constantly struggling) business. You might be a student, a school leaver or a stay-at-home parent.

Furthermore, this concept applies regardless of what you are trying to achieve. You might be seeking a promotion, or your first job. You might be trying to restart your career after taking a break to look after children, or after illness, or redundancy.

Alternatively, your ambition might have nothing to do with work or career. You might be looking for a new partner, or a new interest, or a new way to express yourself. Or you may be a creative person whose creativity has fallen into the doldrums for one reason or another. The principles at play here will work in every circumstance.

Imagine a horizontal line, as shown below. We'll call the left-hand end of this line 'weak' and the right-hand end of the line 'strong'. As you'll have already guessed, this is not a measure of physical strength but of brand strength.

Where would our old friends Apple be on this line, or Coca-Cola? Well, a good long way to the right. In fact, Coca-Cola, generally recognized as the most powerful brand in the world, would be at the very far end of the line, while Apple, which established itself in the early years of the 21st century as the world's 'most admired' brand, would be pretty close behind.

Weak   **Strong**

What about negative publicity, of the kind received by brands when they are involved in some kind of crisis, like BP and the Gulf of Mexico Disaster in 2010? Or the long-term negative publicity about a range of health and environmental issues connected with McDonald's? Or the changing fortunes of the British Royal Family for that matter, depending on behaviours of individuals and their exposure in the media? Well, on this very simple measure we'd put all of these (despite a plethora of negative publicity) at the right-hand end of the line because they are all incredibly famous. Actually, it is more than merely being famous that puts all these brands at the right-hand end of the line. It is because their audiences (and very big audiences they are too, because they are 'global' brands) share a fairly small and well-defined set of meanings.

Even though all the brands mentioned above have now added their share of negative meanings to their 'meaning set' they are nevertheless still fairly well understood as brands by their audiences, and thus still very powerful/strong.

Our set of meanings about these brands hasn't changed that much. Whatever we thought about BP, and whatever we thought about oil companies in general, its importance as a huge UK business hasn't altered markedly. McDonald's still draws diners in their hordes and the British Royal Family remains an historic institution drawing media attention and visitors from across the world.

So, to get back to our theoretical line of brand strength, let's think about what it takes to be at the opposite end: the weak brand end. Well, it is much more difficult, almost by definition, to name a famous business that sits at the left-hand end of the line. More difficult, but not impossible, and the sad demise of the UK store Woolworths is a good example. Woolworths' problem was not lack of fame or profile – there was a branch on virtually every high street in Britain. But Woolworths' set of meanings had become so blurred, so diluted and so muddled, that modern consumers couldn't form a clear picture in their minds about what the brand meant. Over a period of decades, Woolworths slipped along the line from far right to far left.

Also at the far left of the line are many independent shops, cafés and other small and medium-sized businesses. They struggle and then close, and their owners, so full of hope and energy at the start of their enterprise, are left brokenhearted, and often plain broke, when the sign comes down and the whitewash goes up inside the windows. There are a great many reasons why new businesses fail. Brand is only one of them, but it is a much more common factor than most people acknowledge. I think so many of these small enterprises fail not because the product or service they offer is not intrinsically good or desirable, but because they fail to establish quickly and decisively enough a set of authentic, distinctive, compelling and 'excellent' meanings in the minds and hearts of their customers.

ESTABLISHING MEANING

Those businesses that do establish meaning, no matter how small their ambitions might be, are the ones that tend to succeed. And so it is with individuals. Whether you're looking for a job, or a promotion, or a date, you are more likely to succeed if you can establish 'meaning' and therefore pull yourself along the line in the right direction.

Up until the summer of 2008 I would have put myself on the far left of the line. That's not to say that I hadn't achieved anything in career terms – after all I was the co-owner of a medium-sized advertising and design agency, with my name over the door – but as a 'brand' I was still weak in a number of ways.

On a superficial level my skills and abilities were known only to a limited number of people. I had long had the idea of writing a book about creative-thinking strategies, but couldn't get a publishing deal or a literary agent. My decade's worth of experience in advertising was not with a famous agency in London or New York, and when I left the agency of which I was part owner to run my own one-man consultancy, I still had no profile beyond the business boundaries of my city and county.

On a more profound level I was a 'weak' brand because I hadn't created a set of brand meanings for myself, let alone for my other audiences. In other words, I hadn't really considered what I wanted to achieve in any real sense and hadn't shaped any kind of strategy (we'll talk more about creating a strategy a little later).

The turning point for me was when I met with an artist's agent with the aim of getting work as a TV presenter and conference speaker. He said one rather profound thing to me, which was simply that, while I was a competent presenter, I did not have anything distinctive about myself as a 'brand'.

This was not only profound, but something of a shock. I had spent several years advising companies and organizations on brand strategy and here was a flippin' artist's agent telling me that I didn't have a brand! I was hurt. I was a bit cross. And I was shaken. It was a good job, too. He was absolutely right. There was nothing about me that would have given anyone in TV, or anyone looking for a conference speaker, or come to that a publisher, anything to inspire or excite them. I was just another middle-aged ex-advertising guy wanting to shift career. So what?

The agent, to whom frankly I will always be grateful, asked me to 'sell' myself to him face to face. It was deeply intimidating. I explained that I was an expert on brands and branding. The word 'expert' was very dull, we agreed. To cut a long story short we settled on a word, which at the time both embarrassed and excited me: guru. Embarrassed because it is a word that is scorned in so many arenas, and particularly in the field of marketing. Everybody likes a bit of guru bashing. Frequently it is justified, if only because people can take themselves and their knowledge much too seriously.

So I was embarrassed, but I was also excited, because I had a strong hunch we might be on to something. Guru is a Sanskrit word meaning 'teacher', though it clearly has a much greater resonance with many people. I was already running workshops and 'training' client teams in brand and associated topics, and I had ambitions to write a simple guide to branding, so perhaps it was (sort of) descriptive. But much more important was its outrageousness. To use the word guru in a description of oneself is so self-assured as to be obviously a little tongue in cheek.

So, within a few hours of this meeting, I renamed my consultancy from the very ordinary Simon Middleton Company to the potentially risky Brand Strategy Guru.

The effect was dramatic and fast. This simple but bold change of name began to shift me, with gathering momentum, from the far left of the weak-strong line towards the right. Just a few years on, I appear regularly on national television commenting on brands, and speak and consult all over the world. It's worth noting that without that name change I don't think I would have won the commission to write my first book, *Build A Brand In 30 Days*. It was my 'brand' that gave my agent the confidence to make a case to the publisher, and which intrigued the publisher enough to take the outline proposal seriously.

CREATING MEANING CHANGES EVERYTHING

Of course, it is hard to be precise about why such substantial changes happened but I think there are two very particular and equally important reasons. First, the new name of my consultancy obeyed the four principles of branding and therefore made it easy to get my intended meaning into the minds of my desired audiences. It is authentic (I specialize in brand strategy). It is highly distinctive (not only because of its self-confidence, but because of its specificity). It is compelling (it makes an emotional impact: people are either amused, annoyed or engaged by it). And it clearly speaks of excellence (no one but a fool would call themselves a 'guru' unless they were pretty confident of their expertise).

But there's another more subtle and more profound reason for its success. In changing the name of my company, it changed the way I thought about myself. Despite my initial embarrassment at describing my business and myself as a guru, I got used to it and that process is helped along each time I get hired. It seems to be something of a self-fulfilling prophecy therefore, and this is an important element.

My role now is to help others benefit from my experience and I want to help you to create your personal brand, not only because of its effect on your external audiences, but because of its potential to have a profound and positive effect on your view of yourself.

Speaking of positive effects, it's time to add a new dimension to our simple brand benchmark model. We started with a horizontal line from weak to strong, but, as we have noted with BP and other major brands, strength can't be the only measure of a brand. We're now going to add a vertical line to our horizontal to create the figure below.

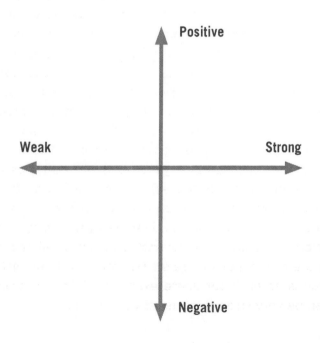

The vertical line goes from positive at the top to negative at the bottom. Now we've got a much more interesting model to map brands upon. Where would you put BP now? Or McDonald's? Or the British Royal Family? Strong? Certainly. But negative or positive? You decide. And have a think about some other familiar brands. Microsoft? Nokia? General Motors? Let's think about countries: they are brands, too. What about the UK or the USA? Russia? Libya? Afghanistan? Almost by definition, 'famous' countries can generally be considered to be 'strong' brands, but they are not always positive.

I spoke recently at a tourism conference in a small Eastern European country much loved by its people and known for being a lovely place for a holiday by its neighbouring countries. It's friendly and pretty, and history, scenery and skiing are just a few of its attractions. Yet the country's tourist industry knows that it has one big problem: simply that it has a very weak-positive brand. It's positive because the people who know it like it. But it is weak because not enough people have a strong set of meanings about the place - either because they don't know it exists, or it doesn't resonate with them. To put it another way, it doesn't mean anything to them.

By contrast, think of poor, blighted Afghanistan. All around the world the name conjures up strong images. Arguably, it has one of the highest profiles of all countries. But is it positive? Tragically, the answer of course is an emphatic 'no'. That could all change in the future. Let's hope so. But for now Afghanistan stands as an unfortunate example of how a 'brand' can be very strong but negative.

Having a weak-positive/strong-negative brand is true of businesses large and small; and as with businesses so with individuals, too. My brand, before the name change, was weak-positive, which is to say that my clients generally thought I did a pretty good job, but I was fairly invisible. This not only hampered my business ambitions, but also my personal growth.

EXERCISE 3: PLOT YOUR BRAND

This exercise is very simple. I'd like you draw a cross and place your personal brand in the appropriate place.

If your brand is somewhere in the top right-hand corner of the cross (strong-positive) then hearty congratulations - you've done fantastically well and your focus should be on staying there. Don't stop reading though, because it is as important to analyse success as it is failure, and you need to constantly consider what makes your brand strong and positive.

And if you're anywhere else on the grid don't despair, this book is all about taking you into a strong-positive position.

The most challenging place to be by far (surprisingly, you might think) is the bottom right: strong-negative. If you have a strong but negative set of meanings then you need to think very hard about the reasons why. What this means is that your audiences share a strong set of meanings about you (hurrah!) but those meanings are, in part at least, negative ones (boo!). My advice here is very simple: focus on what is negative. Analyse it, address it, face up to it and correct it. Whatever you do, however, please don't give up on this project. Regardless of whether the negative meaning is of your own doing, or caused by circumstances, or relates to something about you that is misunderstood, or held against you through prejudice, it can be changed through this project and by following the steps in this book.

Wherever you are starting from I believe that your life can only be improved by the discipline of honestly examining what you mean to the world and why. And that's as good a summary of what brand is about as anything else.

So, don't be afraid: place yourself honestly on the grid. And try to consider the 'degree' to which you consider yourself strong or weak, positive or negative. In other words, rather than just plonking an 'X' in one of the four sections of the chart, try to think about whether you are very strong, or mildly positive, and so on, to give yourself a specific place.

You might also, although it's not vital, wish to place other people or other brands on the chart. Perhaps people you admire (or not). Work colleagues (or rivals perhaps), or other small businesses. Whatever gives you a sense of the particular world in which you live and work. And write the date next to your 'X', because we'll be coming back to this exercise again later.

NEEDS, WANTS, AMBITIONS AND PURPOSE

In the early notes for this book this chapter was called 'What do you actually want from your life?' Put like that the question, depending on how you say it, can sound a little aggressive, or overly dramatic. So instead, in an un-dramatic way, we're going to look at needs, wants, ambitions and purpose.

This is a book about changing your life, and perhaps its most important and fundamental principle is that only 'You' can really know how you want to make that change, in what direction and to what extent. You might want to make a rather modest adjustment to your life – to improve your prospects at work for example, or to stand out a little from the crowd when it comes to applying for a job or winning an interview.

On the subject of interviews, incidentally, I have just heard a story about a small, local (though very good) design company that advertised for a mid-level graphic designer. They received more than 200 applications and, after interviewing numerous candidates, they appointed a designer from Hong Kong whom they had interviewed on Skype. It's a really tough world out there for new design graduates – along with everyone else – especially when they have to compete with applicants from the other side of the world.

So perhaps you are a talented graphic design graduate struggling to get your first role, or a young retail assistant with a dream of starting your own business. Maybe you just really need to find a job, any decent job, after a long period of unemployment. Or maybe you want to get a partner or spouse.

All of these things involve needs, wants, ambitions and purpose, and you need to examine and be clear about all four of them as they apply to you.

If you've ever studied sociology or psychology, at almost any level, you will probably have come across Abraham Maslow and his 'hierarchy of needs', published in 1943 and often portrayed as a pyramid with physiological needs, such as food and water, at the bottom and self-fulfilment, such as career, at the top. It is a theory now largely seen as dated and very limiting but I mention Maslow only to be clear that I am not talking about any kind of hierarchy but rather, and more simply, about separating out our needs, just to make them easier to study. One of these types we are actually going to call 'needs' and the others are 'wants', 'ambitions' and 'purpose'.

Needs

In a sense these are the simplest of your four needs to think about. They have a very real, gritty quality to them. Here are just a few examples.

If you're of working age and haven't got a job, and need to improve your living standard above the minimum, then your prime 'need' will be to find a job or another way of generating income.

If you've been for interview after interview and failed to land roles for which you are appropriately skilled or qualified, or would at least be as good as the next person, then your 'need' is to make sure that at the next interview you cut through in some way.

If you've been consistently unlucky in love, either dating and being dropped, or failing to secure dates at all, then maybe your 'need' is to discover and address what it is that's not quite working with your prospective partners.

If you're good at your job but consistently passed over for promotion, then maybe your 'need' is to look at yourself from the point of view of those responsible for making promotion decisions and to think about what they see when they see (or fail to notice) you.

If you've been struggling to begin, or to make success of, a business enterprise of some kind, then your 'need' is to gain sufficient clarification about what is going wrong in order to decide how to get it right next time, or (just as validly) to make the decision that you are not really an entrepreneur and thus 'need' to focus your energies elsewhere.

All of these 'needs', and the process of thinking and looking at them honestly and objectively, are directly reflective of the kind of process that goes on inside companies when they look at their brands. For a business, a simple 'need' might be to sell more products, or to sell the same number of products at a higher price, or to break into new markets, or to stand out on the supermarket shelf, and so on.

When you reach the end of this chapter, I'd like you to think about your actual 'needs' for a few moments, and make a note of them.

Wants

'Needs' and 'wants', which you might also call desires, are qualitatively different from each other. One is not necessarily more important than the other but they are different.

Marketers and others working with brand names recognize this difference. Needs, which we've already looked at, have the quality of being unavoidable. We all know when we hear the word 'need' that we are hearing about something with an imperative attached to it. We need to eat. We need to pay our rent. We need to get some treatment when we are ill.

For marketers, needs are appealingly simple: consumers need toothpaste, they need bread, they need insurance, they need transport, they need fuel, they need undertakers. But the line between needs and wants is a blurred one.

We might, conceivably, argue that we need a mobile phone, but that isn't the same as wanting a particular brand of phone. The giant Finnish mobile company Nokia, which still sells more mobile handsets than any other manufacturer, has realized recently that people still need mobile phones but that they no longer 'want' Nokias as they once did. Despite huge sales, the company is in severe decline because of the changing 'wants' of its once taken-for-granted customers. In early 2010 Nokia's new American CEO, Stephen Elop, announced that the brand was 'standing on a burning platform', the clear message being that time was running out. A few days later Nokia announced that it was teaming up with Microsoft to develop new products. And though it didn't say so in so many words, what it will be working on is finding something that consumers will actually 'want' rather than just need.

To marketers, then, needs are not enough: wants are crucial, too.

And this matters to you as an individual for two reasons. First because you have 'wants' of your own. And second (which we will come back to later), because your prospective employers, potential partners, customers and so on have 'wants', too. Part of my objective is to help you get to a place where what they 'want' is you!

Let's think about some possible 'wants' and what characterizes them as 'wants'.

You might 'want' to feel more appreciated for what you do in your workplace. You might 'want' to feel at the end of each day that you have achieved something positive, modest or grand, but something that you can consider and say with some pride, 'I did that today'. You might 'want' to have someone to share a conversation with when you go home, someone to go to the cinema with, someone you can call a companion. You might, simply, 'want' to feel loved. You might 'want' to break out of a cycle of repeated negative behaviours connected to drugs or alcohol, or gambling, or abusive or otherwise unhappy and destructive relationships. You might 'want' to like yourself better: to feel pride in some aspects of who you are. You might 'want' to be free of being bullied at school or ignored at work.

These examples, diverse as they are, have one thing in common – they have a high degree of emotional resonance. The things we 'want', in the sense that I am using the word, are the things that we care about; they are things about which we have (sometimes heart-achingly powerful) feelings.

'Wants' can be extremely closely related to 'needs', of course. The 'need' to get a new job after redundancy in order to earn money, for example, is closely entwined with the deep 'want' to get a job in order to restore self-confidence and self-esteem.

On the other hand, they can be completely separate issues. I have met many people with perfectly good jobs that met their needs, but who desperately wanted to be doing something else. The job met the 'need' for security, but not the 'want' for a meaningful activity.

By the way, don't get too hung up about the words here: you hear people use the words 'want' and 'need' pretty much interchangeably every day. I'm not trying to make some kind of semantic point. The important thing is to separate them because they impact on our lives in different, though related, ways.

Don't be afraid of those wants: there's nothing wrong with wanting something. Human society has progressed at least in part because of wants. Nobody 'needs' art or music after all, but we humans 'want' it! Despite the old saying, perhaps it's not just necessity that is the mother of invention. Or, if necessity is the mother, maybe curiosity (wanting to find out for the sake of finding out) is the father.

Before you rush to record your 'wants' and 'needs', take the time to read the next sections, about ambitions and purpose.

Ambitions

Have you ever heard someone described as 'ambitious', or even 'overambitious', or as having 'ideas above their station'? Of course. Ambition is a strange concept, or at least we seem to have a strange relationship with ambition. On the one hand, we admire ambition, with its implied striving to achieve something of note. A young school student's mother might say of her child: 'Oh, she's very ambitious, she's determined to get good grades and study medicine.' And that, of course, is admirable.

On the other hand, we are just as likely to be critical, even judgemental, about anyone who we see as being too ambitious. Sometimes we associate ambition with a certain sort of ruthlessness: 'He was very ambitious – he didn't stop until he owned the company and he didn't care that he trampled on other people to get there!' And sometimes we see ambition as misguided or foolhardy, expressing a kind of hopeless dream: 'I know you want to be a dancer/singer/actor/writer, but do you really think that's realistic?'

But we're not going to make value judgements about ambitions – except in so much as I believe they are a core part of human nature. Humans have always had ambitions; they have always set their thoughts, hopes and dreams on attaining something just out of reach of the everyday: something that requires that one strives for it. Perhaps it is the act of striving that we are somehow born to engage in, and ambition is simply the object of our striving. I don't know, but what I do know is that ambition is healthy and positive. I would go so far as to say it is necessary.

You may have been asked the popular interview question 'Where do you see yourself in two/three/five years' time?' It's arguably not much use as an interview question (there are so many things about conventional job interviews that aren't much use), but the fact that it gets asked so often is significant. As is the fact that so many people find it so hard to answer.

It gets asked because the interviewers are trying to get some sense of the human beyond the suit and the nervous posture. They are trying to see the real person, because our ambitions say something profound about us. I think, however, it is so hard to answer because when we're in an interview situation we don't respond to it as the profound question that it is. We presume (probably correctly, depending on the skills and integrity of the interviewer) that they are seeking a particular type of answer, one that reflects our commitment to their organization.

I've been asked the same question and, although I have been tempted to answer, 'Well, not here mate, that's for sure', I've never had the courage to do so. Of course not, I'd be out the door and I don't think I'd be getting the job!

But if you imagine for one second that the question can be taken at face value and that it's a genuine, non-judgemental attempt to understand a bit more about you as a person, then how would you answer?

Remember my interview for the mechanic's apprenticeship. I don't think they asked me the 'where do you see yourself?' question but if they had, I hope I would have had the courage to say that I saw myself as an up-and-coming Grand Prix driver. They may still have shown me the door, but perhaps, just perhaps, they might have appreciated my bold ambition, invited me to stay in touch and encouraged me to take certain steps to prove my commitment to my dream. Instead, they didn't ask, I didn't answer and my ambition was uncovered as a kind of guilty secret.

And that's the nub of the matter: I want to utterly dispense with the notion that ambition should in any way be considered awkward, embarrassing, vulgar, foolhardy, childish or silly.

I think there is a very real sense in which you can't move forwards without ambition. So now I want you to think about yours.

Your ambitions will tend to have a different quality from your 'wants'. Whereas 'wants' might be said to be strongly associated with emotions, ambitions are more to do with doing something, or becoming something, or striving towards something.

If you have ever watched any of the TV talent competitions such as The X Factor, you will have heard many of the performers talking about their dreams of pop stardom. If you watch enough of these shows, and particularly the early episodes of each series, before the focus shifts away from the open auditions, you will notice a curious thing – so many competitors seem to be describing a real ambition (to become a pop singer), but something about their tone and their manner indicates that it's not really ambition at all: it is 'want'.

Many of the competitors don't have an ambition to be a professional singer: instead they want, often very badly, to be famous, to be loved, to be respected, even to like themselves more.

And it also fascinates me how one can spot the individuals who not only have genuine talent, but also genuine ambition.

Now all this might sound like I'm an advocate of this kind of show as a means of discovering and encouraging musical talent. I'm not actually, and, on balance, I'm rather anti it, for the simple reason that I think the hurt it does to the deluded many outweighs the good it does for the talented/ambitious/lucky few. Nevertheless, I do believe that some of the winners of the show exhibit the quality of genuine ambition in the sense that I want you to understand it.

Perhaps you could think of ambition as a dream that you're prepared to work at: and for 'work at', read 'sweat, sacrifice, suffer and strive'!

Another way to identify ambition is the longevity of the dream. My motor-racing dreams lasted only a couple of years. Probably not a real ambition at all. Did I work to prove that I was dedicated to the dream? Did I do everything in my power to race karts (the way in for so many young drivers)? Did I nag my parents endlessly to take me to races? Well, the honest answer is 'no'.

By contrast, did I ever stop writing in one way or another from my early teens? I did not. Did I spend long hours, when I could have had any other hobby, writing poems and stories, most of which would never (quite rightly) see the light of day? Absolutely. That was a proper ambition. See the difference?

So, when you get to the exercises at the end of the chapter, I want you to think big (as big as you like). Don't be afraid of your dreams. But I also want you to think about which of your dreams are actually ambitions in the sense that we're talking about.

The best advice I ever received referred to ambition. A very smart acquaintance of mine, with whom I did a small branding project, asked me at the end of our short time of working together if I would mind him giving me some advice. He said: 'Don't limit your ambitions: there are plenty of people out there who will happily do that for you.'

He wasn't being cynical, but rather he was detecting (rightly) that there was something about me that was not fulfilling its potential. It was a liberating moment. This was a professional for whom I had immense respect. Without that comment I doubt, to be honest, that you would be reading this book now.

By the way, ambitions don't have to relate to your working life. My parallel ambition from my teens was to sing in a band. Today I do, and it's a great band; we play some superb gigs at festivals and on the acoustic-roots circuit. But it's not my profession: it's artistic endeavour (we like to say) but it's not work. There was a time when I wanted to be David Bowie, and then Bob Dylan and then Joe Strummer and then Bruce Springsteen. But I'm over it now. Now I want to be in a band for the pure pleasure of it, playing with skilled fellow musicians (much better musicians than me as it happens) and I'm prepared to work at it to make sure it's the best band it can be!

Purpose

You can see purpose come to life any day of the week – if you look in the right places. You can see it on the faces and in the behaviour of real statesmen and women.

You might say (well, I would) that Barack Obama didn't just have an ambition to become President of the United States of America: you might reasonably say that it was his life's purpose. You can see and hear in the keynotes of Steve Jobs that his purpose was to make Apple a great company with every product and every year, and every new customer. I watched a documentary film recently about the American singer-songwriter Ron Sexsmith – an interesting figure with an 11-album career who is much admired by other better-known artists such as Paul McCartney and Elvis Costello, and with songs recorded by big stars like Michael Bublé.

Nevertheless, Sexsmith had, until 2011, failed to make the kind of commercial breakthrough that would allow him to be secure financially, and to feel like the years of craft and sacrifice had been worthwhile. In recent years, he has considered quitting the business altogether. But he persisted because, to paraphrase his fiercely admiring wife, he was 'born' to write songs. He commented himself that he felt he could be a better person in his songs than he could be in real life. What a profound and moving recognition and expression of purpose! Happily (because his songs and voice are beautiful and distinctive), Sexsmith seems finally to be breaking through to a much bigger audience.

But purpose is not the exclusive province of presidents, CEOs and creative artists. My wife was a general nurse for many years. And, though I have no wish to embarrass her, she is a good, modest example. Her purpose in those years was simply to be the 'kindest' nurse. I know from her attitude, and from the numerous comments of others, that she was unrivalled in the simple purpose of providing super-kind super-caring. It's a modest enough purpose, but it is also profound.

I have known teachers of 'challenging' children whose simple purpose was to engage young people who would otherwise not be engaged.

And in case you think that I'm getting all worthy and pious here, I've known publicans whose clear purpose was to run the best pub anywhere.

YOUR MISSION STATEMENT

Companies frequently have a thing called a 'mission statement'. It is usually a rather dry and dull explanation of what the company is trying to achieve. You can find them on the websites, and framed in the receptions, of most large companies. But mission statements only tend to be dull because they try too hard to be all things to all people and, as a result, they end up being generic and bland. They are not often inspiring but they could be.

The French have the expression *raison d'être*, meaning 'the reason for being'. That's what I mean by purpose. The simple, profound, single-minded reason for all your striving!

The Germans have the expression *schwerpunkt*, meaning 'the point of the spear' or the focus of attention and effort. That's a great way to think about purpose.

For Ron Sexsmith the point of the spear is to write ever more profoundly beautiful and affecting songs. For Steve Jobs the point of the spear was to continually prove Apple's rightful place as the world's leading personal technology company. For Nelson Mandela the point of the spear was to lead South Africa to freedom.

It is important to note that your purpose will not necessarily remain the same forever, at least not in its specifics. People's lives are rarely focused permanently on one area of interest - unless, like Ron Sexsmith, you do one thing so very well that it becomes your life's work. Athletes may become trainers. Actors sometimes become directors. Nurses can become artists.

But, having stated that rather obvious caveat, I would like to ask you to think long and hard about your purpose. Yes, long: ponder it over a walk, or discuss it with someone close to you, or go to sleep with it in the back of your mind, or meditate upon it.

You might, if you have first worked through your needs, wants and ambitions, get a sense that each of these informs and feeds into the next. If you come up with a description of 'purpose' that doesn't reflect your 'wants' and your 'ambitions' in some way, then I suspect you weren't entirely candid with yourself.

EXERCISE 4: NOTING YOUR NEEDS, WANTS, AMBITIONS AND PURPOSE

Needs

Remember that we're talking about the fundamental stuff here. Perhaps think about them as the things you feel are getting in the way of you getting on with your life.

Write a very brief description (no need for an essay), such as 'find a girlfriend', 'get a job', 'make my business profitable', 'give up smoking'. Then give yourself a target date for each 'need'. For some needs that date will be imposed upon you by circumstances, for others there's no fixed date: but set a target. And of course make a note of today's date. You can look back later to see how you've got on.

Wants

You've got the hang of this now. All you're doing here is making a list of the things you 'want' from life. This may seem like a modest enough activity. You may even feel that it's redundant. I promise you, it is anything but. By simply writing or typing out your 'wants', you will be focusing on them, considering them and assessing their importance to you in a way that most people never take the time to do. You will be reflecting in a way that will put you in a strong place when it comes to the later task of creating and refining your personal brand.

And don't be afraid of some of the 'wants' being material. It's absolutely fine to want more money, for example. The thing to keep focused on, however, is the way your wants will make you feel. Again, add a target date and today's date for each 'want'. And remember that wants are different from needs. If you're in any doubt, do look over this chapter again.

Go on then... what do you really want?

Ambitions

Remember, there are just two 'rules' (let's not call them rules, let's call them guidelines) about what constitutes an ambition.

First it will be something that requires you to strive towards it in some way; if you can achieve it without much effort then it isn't an ambition. But that's not to say that striving is the same for everyone. I have known people for whom going to the cinema was an ambition and which, because of their circumstances, was not only a substantially challenging ambition, but also a long-held one.

Second, you are prepared to do the striving. Our earlier definition of ambition was a dream that you're prepared to work for. As we've learned, you don't get to be a Grand Prix driver, or indeed Bruce Springsteen, by just dreaming.

So what are the dreams that you are (really) prepared to strive for? Don't put a target date on these: let's not fence our dreams in too much, eh?

Purpose

Your purpose doesn't have to be expressed in a snappy line and don't fret over language because you're not writing a slogan! It may be that only you will ever see or hear it. But it should be honest and considered, and as focused as you can make it.

One way to think about your purpose is as a summary of both your wants and your ambitions. It will be more general than either. In case it helps at all, I will tentatively share with you what I think of as my purpose in this phase of my life. It is simply as follows:

To take everything I have learned about business and creativity and to turn it into something that can justifiably be called wisdom, which will be valued by individuals and organizations.

See, it ain't a snappy line. It doesn't roll off the tongue. But it means something to me: it is the point of the spear! Your turn now! And remember to sign and date your purpose.

REAL-LIFE REINVENTORS ✦
Louis Barnett: chocolatier and 'devoted conservationist'

Louis Barnett's success is driven by a convincing and engaging personal narrative that creates meaning and adds value to the chocolate he sells. At the age of 11, he was diagnosed with dyslexia, dyspraxia, dyscalculia and short-term memory loss. As a result, he was home schooled and eventually found work at a falconry centre. Asked to make a chocolate cake for his aunt's birthday, Louis found an amazing Belgian chocolate recipe. She loved it and so did everyone else. Further requests for the cake followed, eventually from local delicatessens and restaurants. To meet demand, Louis set up the company Chokolit, making him the UK's youngest entrepreneur at 12, and the youngest supplier to leading supermarkets. Committed to the environment, he banned palm oil from all his products because of its association with the destruction of animal habitats. Within a few years of beginning his enterprise, Louis had become a high-profile ambassador for disability and conservation charities and young entrepreneurship.

Chapter 4

TURNING AMBITION AND DESIRE INTO PERSONAL BRAND STRATEGY

Businesses and organizations talk a great deal about strategy, as do politicians and the military. As a result the word 'strategy' can seem somewhat intimidating and leaves some people thinking that 'strategy isn't for me'. But I would urge you to think about strategy in these very simple terms: a strategy is just a description of where you want to go.

Actually, that is not the conventional description. Many people in business think of strategy as synonymous with planning. In other words, a description of 'how' you are going to get where you want to go and 'what' you are going to do to get there.

But I think that's a much less helpful description. I don't want you to worry about the 'how' and the 'what' for the moment, but instead to focus on the 'where'.

Of course, I don't mean 'where' in a geographic sense, but rather as a description of some kind of 'achievement point' in your career or life journey. It's not the end point of your personal story of course (after all, who knows where the end point is for any of us?). It is something of significance, however, something you might feel deserves to be called a destination.

To use an example from popular culture, think of J.R.R. Tolkien's epic book *The Lord of the Rings,* or the extraordinary trilogy of films by Peter Jackson. Whether or not you're a fan of the story, the chances are that you're familiar with the basic premise: in a long battle between good and evil in Middle Earth, success for the good guys (an alliance of races including humans, elves, dwarves and, of course, hobbits) depends on the destruction of an innocuous-looking gold ring, which is in fact the source of the power of the bad guys.

Early on in the story, and not without lots of rivalry and prejudice getting in the way of the common cause, the alliance of good guys agree that they must destroy said ring of power. Now the particular mythology of the story makes it clear that there is only one way to destroy the ring, which is to drop it back into the volcano (ominously but appropriately named Mount Doom) in which it was originally forged.

And that, to put it simply, is 'strategy'. Destroying the evil ring by popping it back into the volcano. That's the crucial strategic decision taken by the story's key protagonists on which the rest of the narrative is based.

Note that when the strategy (destroy ring in volcano) is agreed, there is no detail attached to it. This is what you might call the 'big picture', but that doesn't make it vague. It's interesting and important to recognize that the strategy is not a more general statement like 'defeat evil' or 'save Middle Earth'. Those ambitions lie behind our heroes' strategy, but they are too vague to be called strategic in themselves, or to be much use as strategies.

And neither, as we've already pointed out, does the strategy of destroying the ring in Mount Doom have a lot of flesh on its strategic bones. It doesn't say who exactly is to have the honour of dropping the evil ring into the volcano, or how they are going to get there. In fact, for those not familiar with the story, the heated debate about who should carry out this task is the turning point of the whole narrative. As pretty much everybody knows, it is the least likely of heroes, a vertically challenged, hairy-footed hobbit named Frodo, who volunteers for the job. But that's not the point. The point is that the big-picture strategy is (just) detailed enough for everyone involved to have a very clear picture of where they are going. But it's not bogged down in the fiddly stuff about who is actually going to do it, when they're going to do it (beyond 'urgently' that is) or (most significantly) how they are going to do it.

STRATEGY

Strategy is about big-picture decision-making – about the big destinations in life, or in career, or business, or self-development, or indeed relationships.

Once you've considered and decided upon your strategy, then you can move on to making plans, which is the bit where you decide when, who, how and so on.

And if you think I'm banging on about this a bit too much, I would like you to consider for a few moments the consequences of not sorting out your strategy first and concentrating instead on the planning bit, or even (which is where so many of us have gone wrong to our cost) actually taking substantial action without having a strategy or planning.

If you take substantial action without having a strategy, then whatever action you take – no matter how bold, skilful or indeed effective you are as an individual or a company – it will be at best a matter of luck as to whether that action achieves the results that are right for you. Let me just repeat that: if you take action without establishing strategy you are relying pretty much on luck.

Maybe, possibly, that sort of approach to life might suit your personality. I'm not saying there's anything wrong at a fundamental level with not living strategically. Of course not: only a total bore, or a psychopath, gets up every morning and consults their 'strategy' to decide how to spend the day. What I am saying is that in order to achieve some kind of substantial change in your life, your business or your career, you do need to consider 'why' you are taking certain actions. And the very act of asking, 'why am I doing this particular thing?' is a strategic act in itself. And to act without asking the question is most probably not going to help you (unless you're just damn lucky) to make the kind of change that your needs, desires and ambitions are pointing you towards.

So, to give you a stark example: if you have no strategy you can make extraordinarily counter-productive decisions. In my late twenties, bored with life in PR, I decided to train as a nurse. Why? Was it because I had long harboured an ambition to be part of the admirable 'caring professions'? No. I wish I could say that I had a vocational calling, but that would be completely disingenuous. I had no calling, and the truth is that I hadn't examined myself (needs, desires, ambitions) sufficiently to allow me to make a strategic decision. As it happened, a lot of my friends were nurses, and my wife Sheila was a nurse (a proper vocational one to boot). It sounded quite nice to me. And it was. But it was still a huge strategic career error.

I actually spent about six years as a nurse, and a few more in the NHS in other roles, and in the years since then I have frequently claimed that the experience was invaluable and all part of the rich tapestry of life. Well, maybe so, but it is also true that I personally have some regrets – not so much for having had that experience, but for the lost opportunities and direction of almost a decade on the wrong career path.

It wasn't a catastrophic decision you might be thinking, but it was a strategic error that took me in the wrong direction. Think of it in terms of navigation and you can see that heading in the caring-professions direction might only have been a couple of degrees off-course, but a decade later that couple of degrees put me in a very different landscape from the one that actually suited my skills and personality.

Practically speaking, I was nearly 10 years older, completely out of touch intellectually and emotionally with the field of marketing and PR, and, in effect, obliged to start from scratch – at the age of 35 – in an industry in which my peers had a decade's more experience.

So, I hope you believe me that strategy matters and, what's more, that it is not complex and technical, but much more about simply taking the time out to think about where you want to go.

And before we move on, let's deal with the difference between strategy and 'objectives'; it's important that we deal with this because so many management and self-help books talk about setting objectives. Specifically, you may well have read or heard about so-called SMART objectives. This rather appealing acronym stands for specific, measurable, attainable, relevant and time-bound.

I have no particular argument with objectives, even SMART ones, but for our purposes right now this definition is too complex and too corporate. I don't think that individual people really, in ordinary life, go round setting themselves SMART objectives. There is something a little soulless about turning our desires and ambitions (our dreams, if you will) into specific, measurable, attainable, relevant and time-bound objectives.

So, instead I'm asking you to do something that is not only as more profound, and somewhat more human and real-world, but also rather easier –

assuming that you give yourself time to really think about the big picture.

EXERCISE 5: IDENTIFYING YOUR DESTINATION

To do the following exercise effectively you'll need to note down again the set of ambitions that you developed in the last chapter. And you'll need to remember that we are describing a big-picture 'destination' or strategy for achieving them.

Remember the good guys in Tolkien's tale? Their ambition and desire, if you will, was simply to live happily and peacefully as they had done prior to the rise of the bad guys. To achieve this they decided that their strategy was to put the ring back into the volcano from which it originated, thus depriving the top bad guy of his power.

So their strategy was more detailed than 'defeat evil' or 'save Middle Earth', but still 'big picture' in the important sense that it didn't worry about who, how, when and so on.

And that's what I am asking you to create now – a strategy that is your own version of 'put evil ring back in volcano'.

Of course, I'm not looking over your shoulder and I can't see exactly what you're writing down, so you will have to be the judge of whether you have created something strategically useful or not. There are a number of questions that you can ask yourself, though, which may help.

But first, have a go, as follows.

Step 1

Note down again your ambitions and desires from the previous chapter.

Step 2

Complete the following sentence:
   My strategy for achieving these ambitions is...

Now ask yourself the following questions:

1. *Does this strategy feel big enough to do the job? Will it achieve my ambition?*

2. *Does it indicate, broadly speaking, that some kind of action is required? Bear in mind though that the 'action' might be, in some circumstances, to remain passive, or to carry on doing what you're already doing.*

3. *Are you left with some unanswered questions about how and when this strategy is going to be achieved? Good, you should be: remember it's a strategy, not yet a plan (we will come to that in good time).*

If your answer to the above questions is 'yes', then you have probably created something that could be called a 'strategy'.

Now I would like you to write this on something that you can keep about your person for the next few months, or even years, because you won't achieve your strategic intent overnight – unless you're extraordinarily lucky or just plain gifted (in which case, you don't need to create a strategy at all and you probably aren't reading this book anyway). You can write it on a scrap of paper of course, but I would recommend something with a little more durability: perhaps a card that you can keep in your wallet or purse, or tucked in the back of your diary. Or maybe you want it loud and proud, stuck on the wall. Whatever suits you.

The important thing is that it serves as a kind of touchstone, a reminder of your direction of travel. And, as you move forwards and grab some opportunities and turn down others and get some good luck and some bad and make good decisions and bad ones, you will be able to remind yourself periodically of where you are trying to get to and why.

Along the way your tactics and circumstances will almost certainly change. Sometimes huge obstacles will be put in your way. At other times you will be simply gripped by a sense that you are not achieving anything at all. It is at these times that this written reminder of your strategy will be of greatest value, because it will provide the answer to the existential question that afflicts us all from time to time: 'Why do I bother?'

And it's not just during the tough times that your strategy will be of strength and value, but in the good times, too. It is very easy to get distracted by success, or to lose direction because of positive circumstances; good luck can throw you off course just as effectively as bad luck can block your way.

REAL-LIFE REINVENTORS ♥
Paul Burns: war veteran turned adventurer

For as long as he could remember, Paul Burns wanted to be in the army. Newly recruited and just eight weeks into a tour of duty in Northern Ireland in 1979, a massive IRA bomb destroyed the four-ton truck in which he was travelling. Paul barely survived. His body was broken. His left leg was amputated below the knee. His skin was burned down to the bone. Those who saw him wondered if it might not be kinder to let him die. But Paul refused to be beaten. He had made a promise to himself that he would make up for the loss of his friends' lives by living his own life to the full. He spent a year in hospital, then a year in rehabilitation and has been in constant pain ever since. He refused, however, to let the loss of one leg and severe damage to his other foot rule his life and has gone on to do many things that might daunt fully able-bodied people: freefall parachuting, sub-aqua, motorcycling, skiing and sailing round the world as a member of a disabled crew. 'I really have lived these last 30 years' he says. 'I have tried to fill every day. Tried to make people smile, tried to inspire all around me, and to show the IRA they could not break me.'

Chapter 5

ESTABLISHING YOUR
BRAND VALUES

Companies, brands and organizations of all sizes talk about values all the time. There is a real sense in which the idea of values has become somewhat devalued through overuse.

And the issue of overuse is compounded by the question of whether our values actually make any difference at all to our behaviour. If they don't, then you have to wonder if they are of any use (of any value, in fact). Values can easily become meaningless statements, or even provide a kind of cover for behaviour that is far from admirable. This can be seen most distinctly in the corporate world: big companies frequently lay claim to positive, sometimes even saintly, values, which are hard to criticize. Closer examination, however, can reveal that the business can hardly be said to be 'living by' its espoused values set.

So values have something of a tarnished reputation and it would be quite easy to choose not to pay much attention to them here. Nevertheless, my gut instinct, and my experience of working with brands large and small, is that people still care about values.

WHAT ARE VALUES AND WHY DO THEY MATTER?

A slightly circular answer to that question is that values matter because they, er... matter. In other words, values are concepts that are, to individuals perhaps more convincingly than organizations, of such significance that they guide both thinking and behaviour.

Perhaps it's more helpful to say that values are things which we feel or believe so strongly that we will not compromise about them. In workshops, I have been known to define values as those things that I will 'fight someone in the car park for', which is perhaps not a very adult analogy, but I think you get the idea.

How and why values have developed as part of our humanity I am neither qualified nor sufficiently knowledgeable to say. Neither am I the right person to explain whether values are more or less a question of nature or nurture. For our purposes it doesn't matter. What does matter is that we examine and feel at ease with our values, because they effectively form part of the bedrock of our personal brand, which, after all, is what we are trying to create here.

CREATING MEANINGFUL VALUES

When I worked for an advertising agency, we were very enthusiastic about values. In fact we declared that we were a values-driven business. And we meant that statement as a kind of value in itself. In other words, we were declaring that we weren't just driven by the need/want to make money, but to do so decently, honestly and with a care for the wellbeing of the staff and our clients. It was hugely admirable and founded on the commitment of the genuinely values-driven managing director to make a 'good' company.

One of our values, however, was honesty and, to be perfectly frank, on so many levels the odds are stacked against honesty as a value for an ad agency. Of course I don't mean that the business was fraudulent in any way. What I mean is that stating honesty as a key value for any organization implies an almost superhuman effort to be truthful at all times and we all know that, as Aaron Sorkin's screenplay *A Few Good Men* tells us, sometimes people 'just can't handle the truth'.

It's when there is conflict that your values are tested and, in my experience, very few supplier companies are ever going to risk losing a client or customer by standing fiercely by their avowed value of honesty. In the end, most suppliers tell the customer what the customer wants to hear.

Does that mean that I am lobbying for dishonesty, or that I am such a misanthropic cynic that values don't matter? No, of course not, far from it. What I am suggesting is that we all need to be a little tougher and more demanding with ourselves when it comes to values. I don't want you to end up with a set of values that are meaningless.

AVOIDING THE TRAPS

Values can fall into one of two traps. The first is the trap of generic blandness. There is a way in which honesty fails as a value, at least in our brand-building project, simply because it implies that we are seeking some kind of credit (Brownie points, we might say) simply for deciding not to be dishonest. And our decision not to be dishonest, reassuring in one sense, is hardly massively distinguishing. This is simply because you won't find many people proudly claiming to be otherwise, unless, perhaps, they are applying to join the Mafia (and even then that particular organization doubtless demands honesty within its own parameters).

And the second trap into which people fall when considering and declaiming their values is that of committing to a value that is simply going to be too difficult to live up to in the scary world known as 'real life', which, as we all know, is an environment designed to test us on a minute-by-minute basis. That is not to say that values should not be aspirational in some way. Perhaps the striving towards the good itself is something that enhances our personalities, perhaps even our 'souls', but if our values concepts are so aspirational that we are constantly in a state of struggle in trying to live up to them, then perhaps we are better to face up to the fact that they aren't of much use as values to underpin our personal brand.

So, in short, honesty, while generally speaking a good thing, falls at both fences. It is both somewhat bland and rather too aspirational, and therefore not much help as a value in a practical sense.

Which is a rather roundabout way of saying that I urge you to base your personal brand on a set of values that fulfil the following criteria, which you will recognize from an earlier chapter.

Authentic

Establish values that genuinely reflect your personality and the things you care about. Ask yourself the tough question: 'Am I prepared to stand by this value and not compromise because it speaks of me as an individual and is very, very important to me?' If the answer is a confident 'Yes', then perhaps the concept you are considering might just make it as a value. A word of caution here though: even if something is powerfully 'authentic' to you, it does not necessarily mean that you should state it as a value.

You may, for example, be driven by a deep-rooted religious, political or philosophical conviction. I respect that absolutely but urge you to think long and hard before making that conviction an overt value in respect of your 'brand' – either as an individual developing a career or as a business. I once had a business connection with a small firm that repaired computers, but based its brand message around the strongly held religious faith of the proprietors. With no disrespect to the individuals or their faith, in my view their values didn't have much to do with the service they were providing and that for many customers it was off-putting and limiting to their business.

Of course there are circumstances in which faith issues are highly relevant in terms of brand, such as foods that obey religious dietary rules. So I am not saying that you should not base your overt brand values on faith: only that you should consider the effect of doing so on your 'brand' (personal or business).

Distinctive

Consider whether your chosen values are sufficiently distinctive and make sure they aren't 'flabby'. I had a forceful exchange with a participant in a brand workshop for a large charity a few years ago, over his insistence on the concept of 'quality' as a value. He wanted to know what was wrong with 'quality' as a value. I said, somewhat bluntly perhaps, that it was dull. He came back with the passionate argument that quality was at the centre of everything. I responded that I certainly hoped so. He wanted to know why, in that case, I was arguing against it being part of their values set, to which the simple and truthful response was that I have yet to meet an organization (commercial, public or charitable) which didn't claim that quality lay at the heart of everything they do. And they may well all be right, but the fact that everybody claims it pretty much knocks it on the head as a valuable value.

Let me give you a counter example. I spend quite a lot of my working life speaking at conferences, and one of the core values of my professional brand is to be 'highly engaging'. Now at first hearing that might seem slightly odd as a value statement – surely it goes without saying that a conference speaker ought to be engaging? Well you'd think so, wouldn't you, but many conference speakers are actually a bit, well, dull. One of the most common crimes is overuse of PowerPoint or other presentation software. I rarely use it because my commitment is to be 'highly engaging', and PowerPoint so frequently leads to sleep.

Coupled with this is another of my brand values: being 'grounded'. In other words, my presentations are not big dramatic affairs in which delegates are asked to punch the air in order to demonstrate their motivation. Curiously, conference organizers are as wary, in my experience, of what is sometimes known as the 'ra ra' approach as they are of 'death by PowerPoint'. So my linked values of being 'highly engaging' and 'grounded' make a distinctive and appealing combination.

Compelling

To be compelling as a brand means, as discussed earlier, to make some kind of impact on your audience, whether intellectual, emotional, sensory or otherwise. With this in mind then, we need our values to be compelling, too. The worst response you can get to a values statement is 'so what?' And what makes a compelling values statement? One that has clear implications about behaviour.

Let's say you run a small shop, and one of the values that you hold dear is to deliver exceptional customer service. Well that's what you need to tell people. Not just 'customer service', but 'exceptional customer service'. That's compelling. That's worth saying – and of course it implies behaviour, which you then have to deliver.

You hear so many companies these days talk about their 'green' credentials in one way or another. The last time you stayed in an hotel, you might have seen a little card in the bathroom asking you to put used towels in the bath and hang the ones you'll use again on the rail. That's fair enough, but it's frequently tied up with a values claim which implies, 'that way you'll be helping us to save the planet', which just rings hollow. Do you believe that most hotel chains have 'saving the planet' high on their agenda? I don't.

But I'm not arguing against making concern for (and action on behalf of) the environment part of your value system. I'm just saying that you need to pursue the thought further in order to come up with a value that is genuinely compelling and impacts on your behaviour. It's for you to decide what it is.

There's a word of caution here, too, which is, as with my earlier point about faith-based values, there is always a danger of painting yourself into a philosophical corner. Choose values that have clout, but avoid those which restrict your ability to run your business, or to do your job!

Excellence

Whatever your purpose and ambition, remember that all your audiences (employers, customers, potential partners) are looking for something, too. And what they're looking for is something life-enhancing in whatever way is appropriate to them.

What this means for you and your values is that you should be orienting yourself towards excellence. And excellence is not the same as perfection.

I've interviewed people – and worked for others – who have stated vehemently that they are perfectionists. In some cases they overtly said that perfectionism is one of their values; in others it is something of a quiet (and sometimes not so quiet) obsession. But I instinctively steer clear of the perfectionists because, instead of pointing towards excellence, perfectionism just seems to point at itself. Perfectionism is too dogmatic to be a useful value for an individual or a business, too judgemental and too wrapped up in itself.

So my advice is to choose a value that points towards excellence, instead of trying to define excellence. Exceptional commitment to hard work – that's a value I can buy. Openness to learning is another. Willingness to listen. Utter reliability. Do these sound like values to you? I hope so, because they are clearly things that will be valued by others (customers, employers, partners) and they have clear implications for behaviour. And, critically, they point towards excellence without boxing you in.

Now you choose.

EXERCISE 6: IDENTIFYING YOUR VALUES

With that preamble in place you'll have guessed what's coming next. I'd like you to make a list of your values. Make a long list first then review it and think about value, asking yourself whether it truly, genuinely resonates with you. Can you live by it? Can you match up to it? Will anyone else care, or is it bland and generic? Is it authentic, distinctive and compelling? And does it point towards excellence?

Long list

For the long list, you don't need to sweat too much over the precise words. Just capture your first thoughts.

The real values list

Now comes the real challenge. I think three or four values are all anyone needs to talk about. Better to have a small set of powerful, behaviour-changing values than a long list of bland statements.

Make a short statement under each of the values in your shortlist. Simply say what this value means in practical, real-world terms.

Let's say one of your values is 'exceptional customer service'. You'll want to say what it actually 'means' in terms of what you 'do'. It doesn't have to be an essay, but it does need to bring the value to life in some way.

Please don't regard this exercise as a chore. Writing down your three or four 'values' and their 'meanings' will really help to embed them, and you'll find it easier to call them to mind later, when the need arises.

REAL-LIFE REINVENTORS ❗
Siza Mtimbiri: scholar and HIV campaigner

Siza Mtimbiri was born in a poor, rural area of Zimbabwe and was one of seven siblings. Growing up, HIV was a constant threat within his community and it wreaked a heavy toll on his family. He lost brothers, nephews and cousins to the disease. At the age of 10, after Zimbabwe became independent, Siza's family decided to buy a plot of land in a whites-only area. He describes this as 'a defining moment' in his life as, until that time, he had received only the most basic primary education. He was the only black child at his new school and about 18 months behind the other children. He soon caught up though, and had other educational chances, which propelled him to universities in South Africa, Morocco, the USA and the UK. Siza received the prestigious Gates Cambridge scholarship to study his PhD at Cambridge University and later founded a charity called Hope Academy and Medical Center, which campaigns for education and healthcare in Zimbabwe's rural communities.

Chapter 6

PUTTING YOUR PERSONAL BRAND IN CONTEXT

This chapter, I promise, is going to be a bit of a toughie, simply because I will be asking you to think about what I'm going to refer to as 'the competition'.

In business and marketing environments, the competition is something that is constantly monitored and discussed by companies, from the largest multinationals to the smallest local businesses. Your window cleaner wants to know what his or her competitors are up to and what move they might make next, just as acutely as the world's largest brands in telecoms, computing, fashion or anything else. Have you heard of ice-cream wars? Curry wars? Those are extreme (though not uncommon) examples of small businesses that are acutely aware of their competition and taking action, which might range from rounds of dramatic price-cutting to outright sabotage.

Competition is everywhere, as I am always reminding start-up businesses. Many of them think that they don't have any competition at all, or they severely underestimate its significance and the threat it poses. This is virtually only true of start-ups though. You only have to be in business for a matter of weeks to learn very quickly that competitors not only exist, but are also of massive importance. Most 'mature' businesses, small or large, do heed the fact that they have competitors; they don't always respond appropriately, but that's another story.

IT ISN'T ONLY BUSINESSES THAT HAVE COMPETITORS: IT'S ALL OF US

When we apply for a job, get invited for an interview, look for a promotion, or perhaps steel ourselves to ask for a pay rise, we have a tendency to be somewhat blinkered in our view. Two things are usually acutely in focus in these circumstances. The first is the person, or faceless organization in some cases, that we have to impress. The second is ourselves. About either of these protagonists we can have a whole range of thoughts and feelings. We often exaggerate the faults or virtues of either or both parties. We are often, for example, desperately anxious and shy in an interview, or we go to the other extreme and overcompensate, appearing so self-assured as to be perceived as being arrogant. Likewise, it is all too easy to overestimate or underestimate the individual or panel doing the interviewing.

The same can apply to a rather different kind of interview – one which you might call a social or a dating interview. We worry about how we might look or sound to the other person. And we worry about what's going on in their head.

Curiously, however, we rarely seem to give much heed to a third element, one that is present in all of these scenarios: the competition.

Perhaps this is partly because our competitors are frequently invisible until we think it's too late to do anything about them. For instance, we are unlikely to have an encounter with competitors for a new job until we possibly have to sit next to them, uncomfortably, outside someone's office. Of course there are exceptions to this, such as when we are applying for a promotion and we know one or more of our peers is doing the same. Or having to go through the ghastly, but increasingly common, process of reapplying for our own job. And, of course, there are scenarios (let's call them 'romance') in which we may already know the other person (or people) vying for our prize. But even in those circumstances when we can clearly see the competition, we tend, as individuals, not to think much about them. I don't think that's because we regard them as unimportant. Quite the opposite: I think it's because thinking about the competition is potentially scary stuff. And then some...

Somehow the blasted competitor/s always seem to have an edge. So we, like a child hiding their eyes and hoping they can't be seen, have a tendency to pretend that the competition doesn't exist.

This is a mistake, but perhaps not for the reason that you might presume. It's a mistake to ignore the competition, but not because they are bigger, cleverer, better looking, better at interviews and better qualified than you or I, and thus generally more likely to win heart, mind, job, pay rise or date, but because, on examination, it usually turns out that they are none of these things. The competition tends to be pretty much the same as us. They might have a slightly different set of skills or experience, or be slightly better or worse looking. In other words, they as just as likely to get the job, win the promotion or get the date. The important thing is, by being aware that there *is* competition, you can work on creating your own 'edge'.

Our usual 'head in the sand' attitude to the competition is the opposite of that used by established businesses – they tend to obsess about the competition, but the best of them do it with a certain discipline and structure, and we can learn from them in developing a personal brand.

So, the tough truth is that there are virtually always competitors out there. The happy corollary of this truth is that they nearly always suck. Yes, really, and we will look at why shortly. But we can't know that about them for sure unless we give them due consideration.

One of the key ways to get a grip on the competition (and remember, this applies to all aspects of life, not just in business) is to divide them up into types. This is also an important process because it ensures that you take account of competitors whom you might otherwise overlook.

Direct competitors

Let's say you run a coffee shop. Your direct competitors are, well fairly obviously, other independent coffee shops but, sadly, it doesn't end there. There are also the big-brand stores such as

Starbucks, Costa, Pret A Manger and so on. These guys are your direct competitors, too. They may be a different size, but they are all direct competitors because they sell pretty much exactly the same thing as you do, in similar circumstances.

Indirect competitors

The direct competition is generally fairly easy to spot, too, although an awful lot of little coffee shop proprietors didn't see the Starbucks phenomenon coming until it was too late. The indirect competition, however, is a little subtler and falls into two sub-types.

First are those businesses who sell similar products, but in slightly different circumstances. Department stores and supermarkets, for example, generally have cafés and restaurants. The larger bookshops have them, too. Although their customers may not be going there with coffee as their priority, they may be inspired to stay and take coffee there rather than coming to find you.

The second sub-type offers something that can be considered a substitute. In the case of a coffee-shop owner, you would count bars and pubs as indirect competitors. You might also include the little mobile coffee carts that are popping up with increasing frequency, serving drinks and snacks to passers-by on the street.

Oblique competitors

I'm going to call the third category of competitor 'oblique', because these are competitors that you may not consider to be competitors at all. To put it simply, oblique competition comes from all of those other opportunities that people have for spending their money, or indeed not spending it. Most people don't have an infinite amount of money to spend on coffee or cakes or anything else that marketing people call 'discretionary', which just means the spending you do after you've paid all your essential bills.

So let's imagine you're a coffee-loving person with a discretionary spend of £10 on any given Saturday afternoon. You might buy a coffee and a pastry while you are pottering about in a relaxed frame of mind, or you might dispose of that money in any number of different ways. You might buy a CD, a book or a couple of magazines, or go to a movie. Anything. Or you might decide to save your money and get your coffee kicks when you get home. Anyway, you take the point: there are any number of things to spend your money on. And that's the oblique competition.

GETTING THE EDGE ON THE COMPETITION

So these are the competitors, but I can hear you wondering, 'How does that help? My coffee shop is doomed!' Now I and other imaginary coffee-shop owners are just depressed.

Well don't be, because by making this single analysis of the competition you have the first step to defeating them: know thine enemy, as they say.

Let me give you a couple of examples. There is a small independent coffee shop in Norwich called The Window Coffee that is not only surviving but thriving, and it's achieved that, it seems to me, by very carefully observing the competition and then outmanoeuvring it. So, instead of trying to compete with the big chains, this little shop focuses on its key strengths of charm and quirkiness. For a start, it tells the immediately engaging story of being 'probably' the world's smallest coffee shop. And it is very small: so small in fact that customers are forced into a kind of intimacy with each other that provides a completely different (and very enjoyable) social experience from any other coffee shop. The effect is much like sitting in a friend's kitchen while they make coffee for you, and this is enhanced by the clever decision of the proprietor not to operate from behind a counter but from in front of it.

It's hard to explain why this feels so different, and so appealing, but it has helped this little business to stand out, create loyal fans and get press and TV coverage way out of proportion to the size of the business, as well as much admiring chatter on social media.

The Window Coffee's brand behaviour isn't big and corporate, or expensive. Neither is it accidental. It is brand behaviour by a proprietor who has thought about and understood her competition but is not intimidated by it. She has ducked and dived around the direct and indirect competition and, by virtue of creating affection and fierce loyalty to her brand, she has sidestepped much of the oblique competition, too.

DEALING WITH THE COMPETITION

So much for the tough world of coffee retail, but how does this model work for everybody else and specifically the individual wishing to win the heart of a new partner, or the job of their dreams?

Precisely the same broad categories of competitor apply in this individual 'marketplace' as in the commercial world. Let's have a look at a few examples.

Imagine you are applying for a job. It doesn't matter what job, but let's assume you have to submit a CV with an accompanying application letter and, if you get through the initial selection stage, you will have to attend an interview.

Before we start worrying about not being qualified for our hypothetical role, or about the impending stress of the even more hypothetical interview, let's think about the competition, in terms of the three broad categories we've established.

The direct competitors are those people with broadly comparable backgrounds, broadly comparable qualifications and skill sets. People a bit like us, in pure job-appropriateness terms.

The indirect competitors are those people who may actually have quite a different profile from the one that the employer appears to require. Perhaps they have different but equivalent qualifications, or are switching from one career path to another. Perhaps they have unrivalled experience, or even very little, but special talents (even gifts) in some related area.

Finally, the oblique competitors are those people who might potentially steal the job from under your nose. This could be someone already in the organization who might get reshuffled, or someone who finds their work expanding to absorb the duties of this job without the need to employ anyone new at all.

In this example, you are applying to a new company and probably have no idea about the individual competitors, but that doesn't matter because we are talking about principles here. The point is that you know what kind of competition you're likely to face. And the question is, how do you deal with them? Well not by panicking, for a start. Again, let's take each in turn. It's not difficult, once you've got these guys sorted out in your mind.

You deal with the direct competition simply by developing a killer brand story for yourself (which we will come to later) that makes you stand out when all other things are equal. Because most, if not all, of the other people of similar qualifications and experience will simply not go to the trouble of creating a brand for themselves. So, by definition, you will have an edge.

You deal with the indirect competition by ensuring that you, like them, have one or two (that's all you need) highly distinctive elements at your disposal to bring to the table. Again, most people simply don't go to the trouble of organizing their thinking in such a way that they utilize elements of their life and experience to offer these highly competitive X-Factor elements. In other words, the elements exist but their stories go untold.

Finally, you deal with the oblique competition in one very straightforward way, which is simply to be aware that such competition exists (the majority are blissfully unaware). This awareness alone will mean that you approach your CV and letter in a different way from most people. In other words, your understanding that the employer may simply decide they might be better off giving the workload to some loyal, longstanding employee will mean (I hope) that you will make sure you know everything it is possible for you to find out about the company, the role, the industry and so on.

EXERCISE 7: THINKING ABOUT THE COMPETITION

The exercise for this chapter will come as no surprise, though, as ever, its value will be determined by the thinking you put into it.

It's in two parts.

First I want you to look at someone or something other than yourself. Pick a company that you admire, or a celebrity, or a sports team, or a writer or musician, or a product. It might even be a city or a country. Or, perhaps, choose an individual, such as a friend or work colleague. The important thing is to choose someone or something about which you feel positive.

Now ask yourself the following questions about your chosen subject and note down your answers, no matter how brief.

- *Who are their direct competitors?*

- *How do they outmanoeuvre their direct competitors?*

- *Who are their indirect competitors?*

- *How do they outmanoeuvre their indirect competitors?*

- *Who are their oblique competitors?*
- *How do they outmanoeuvre their oblique competitors?*

Now think of a scenario, perhaps a challenge of some kind, that you are now facing in a competitive environment. It might be a business challenge if you're an entrepreneur, or want to become one. Or it might be a job or promotion challenge. Or a dating challenge. Anything.

The questions are as before but, this time, you are looking at yourself. Try to be as objective as possible. Don't get too emotional, and at all costs avoid the temptation to be despondent. The whole point about competition is that you are a competitor, too, and you can bet good money that most of the other guys are not bothering to think about things in a disciplined and creative way. That's what will give you the edge!

- *Who are your direct competitors?*
- *How will you outmanoeuvre your direct competitors?*
- *Who are your indirect competitors?*
- *How will you outmanoeuvre your indirect competitors?*
- *Who are your oblique competitors?*
- *How will you outmanoeuvre your oblique competitors?*

REAL-LIFE REINVENTORS ♀

Liz Murray: Harvard graduate, author and international businesswoman

Liz Murray spent her childhood watching her long-term addict parents inject drugs. At first they hid it from her, but as soon as they realized she knew anyway, the door stayed open while they injected their next fix. Any available money from welfare benefits was spent on drugs. Meanwhile, dirty dishes sat untouched in the sink for days and Liz and her sister Lisa rarely went to the park. She recalls that most of the time they lived on egg mayonnaise sandwiches, which they hated, but it got them through the hours when their stomachs burned with hunger. Liz tried hard at school but lack of food and sleep undermined her efforts. Years of truancy, sleeping rough and homelessness followed, but eventually she was given a place at a school that specialized in nurturing underprivileged city kids. She became a straight-A student and went on to Harvard University where she won a scholarship by writing an essay describing obstacles that she had overcome in her life to thrive academically. She graduated in 2009 and is now a motivational speaker and top-ten bestselling author. She also runs her own company inspiring people to change their lives.

Chapter 7

WHO DON'T YOU WANT
TO APPEAL TO?

No one can be loved and admired by everybody, and trying to be all things to all people is a sure-fire way to invisibility and failure. In the world of brands, the big successes are those who are clearly adored by many people, but also have a strong tendency to be disliked intensely by others.

It's a curious truth that one of the most successful strategies in developing a personal brand lies in being very clear about the kind of people (and organizations) to whom you don't want to appeal. I call this 'identifying your brand enemies'. Using the word enemy might sound a little extreme, but I think it's important because I don't want you to have the sneaking thought in the back of your mind that, perhaps after all, you can have universal appeal. You can't. Even if you could, you actually wouldn't want to because it would ultimately weaken your brand.

Universal appeal quickly leads to blandness, and blandness is the death of brand.

The most obvious example from the commercial world is Marmite. This 'delicious' yeast extract product has become the gold standard for things that people either 'love' or 'hate'. The brand has created a long-running marketing campaign precisely around the truth that, while many people adore the taste, many others loathe it with a passion. So successful has this strategy been (precisely because it resonates with a profound human truth) that the idea of something being Marmite-like has entered our vocabulary. Even my house (admittedly quirky), which I love, was described as 'a Marmite house' by the estate agent. Perversely, perhaps, I was immediately even more attracted to the house because of the description.

But Marmite is far from alone in being self-confident about having 'brand enemies'.

Back in the 1980s the early Mac computers from Apple were positioned as 'the computer for the rest of us'. The clear implication of this statement was that Macs were accessible and user-friendly for intelligent and creative people, but were not aimed at 'geeks' or 'nerds'. Apple's enemies at that time therefore were the companies (Microsoft most notably) who oriented their operating systems towards the geeks rather than the ordinary folk, and of course the 'geeks' themselves.

And while Apple is now hugely popular and ubiquitously known, it remains a brand that divides opinion. We Apple fans will barely countenance a word being said against the brand or its products, while its 'enemies' just don't get Apple at all.

I have yet to meet a BMW driver who could imagine themselves owning and driving an Audi, and vice versa. For BMW devotees the 'enemy' are the overly modest Audi drivers who are 'trying too hard to appear not to be showing-off'. BMW, its fans say, is the true driver's car – comfortable with its engineering muscle and in its own, somewhat flamboyant, design skin. Audi fans, on the other hand, think BMW and BMW drivers are a flashy, vulgar bunch and fiercely believe that exceptional engineering can still be discreet.

I'm exaggerating here to make a point, but only a little. And it could be argued that these two monsters of the German auto industry have moved towards each other in recent years: Audi perhaps a little more showy and BMW a little less so. The divide remains, however, and the point still stands – that part of the essence of these brands is their acceptance, even their celebration, of the inevitable fact that not everybody will like them.

KNOW THINE ENEMY

It's important to note that enemy is not just an alternative word to competitor but something rather more profound.

For the Dyson cleaner brand the enemies are not just rival brands, but also its buyers who could only conceive of a conventional cleaner with a bag. Though Dyson's advertisements don't say so explicitly, their implication is clear: if you're not open to technological innovation, which in turn represents 'the future', then this brand is not for you.

There's no actual hostility in this approach to brand thinking, but there is self-assuredness and single-mindedness.

It's a strategy that I have employed with clients and my own brands. My consultancy business is called Brand Strategy Guru, a name, as we've discussed elsewhere, which irritates a few people in the marketing industry. My brand enemies are the stuffy, the straight-laced and the pompous in the industry. My brand name is clearly tongue in cheek, as well as self-assured. It's a deliberately populist name and my enemies are those who want to make branding mysterious (and expensive).

I also have a musical instrument retail business called Left Hand Bear. Guess who the brand enemies are in this case? Yep, no prizes – right-handed people! That's a big group to make an enemy of, but it is actually the strength of the brand, and why it sells guitars, banjos and other instruments all over the world – because it is clearly devoted to the much neglected 13 per cent of musicians in the world who are left-handed.

The real strength of the brand-enemy concept is that it enables you to focus. Take the single example of Left Hand Bear. The enemies are so clear in this case that I am able to focus exclusively on the needs, interests and desires of left-handed players. The prime need for them turns out to be choice. Lefties are constantly facing a problem in music shops, which carry large stocks but only a tiny handful of left-handed instruments. So the Left Hand Bear brand is focused on giving them a choice of high-quality instruments across a range of price bands. It's simple, it's clear and it's focused, which saves a great deal of strategic time-wasting and avoids 'mission drift' (the phenomenon, all too common in business, of starting out trying to do one thing and ending up doing another).

But it's fair to say that the enemy concept can be a dangerous weapon in the wrong hands. Take the idea too far and you can drift into arrogance and alienate everybody. Remember, the idea is to be clear about the people you don't want to appeal to, in order to focus on those that you want to attract.

It is possible to misuse the brand-enemy idea by thinking that everyone is the enemy and behaving accordingly. That's not what I'm advising at all. Please, please don't ever fall into the trap of thinking that developing your personal brand means behaving like an arrogant buffoon. It doesn't.

So now you've got the idea of brand enemies, I want you to start thinking about yours. Remember, this isn't about identifying people whom you like or dislike on a personal basis (although as you go through the exercise that follows you may well see a correlation between your brand enemies and the kind of people who your values and personality lead you to avoid). Instead, this is about developing some clarity of thought, which can help to shape your brand behaviour.

Take a look at the table below, which has some examples of what I am shortly going to ask you to do for yourself.

Brand	Sample Enemy	Reason Why	Resulting Behaviour
Citroën DS3	Fans of 'retro' styling	To be distinct from retro models like Fiat 500, Mini and VW Beetle, and to stay true to the Citroën tradition of stylish and 'modern' design.	Ultra-modern styling and provocative 'anti retro' marketing campaign.
Dave	Old-fashioned TV viewers who think comedy is a just a sporadic reward amongst other programming.	Great comedy is available cheaply, and comedy addicts will happily watch their favourites over and over.	Unapologetic devotion to silliness, with succinct positioning as 'the home of witty banter'.
Dove	Women who believe there is an unachievable 'ideal' look, to which they must aspire.	Because there is a substantial audience open to the Dove message of 'real beauty'.	Using attractive 'real' women in advertising, instead of conventionally glamorous models or celebrities.
Jack Wills	Anyone over the age of 25, plus all the edgy, grungy and more out-there young fashion styles.	Because the 'preppy', 'university' look is (oddly perhaps) highly aspirational.	Bright colours and a relaxed, fresh look, within very tight 'conservative' boundaries.

WHO DON'T YOU WANT TO APPEAL TO?

I am not suggesting, I should add, that any of the brands I've discussed represent an ideal, or indeed that they have necessarily got every element of their brands just right. Very few brands get everything right with absolute consistency all of the time.

What these examples do illustrate is that it is relatively easy to identify, when you start to think about it, the people to whom certain brands are trying NOT to appeal. And this, in turn, gives you a revealing insight into their behaviours.

In each of the cases above we could have given a more detailed list of enemies, which is what I would like you to do. Here's one more example, Richard Branson's Virgin brand, in a little more detail to show you what I mean.

Brand	Sample Enemy	Reason Why	Resulting Behaviour
Virgin	People who think things like air travel and financial services should be serious and corporate.	Because Richard Branson grew up as part of a generation of hippie-rebels and knows there is a rebel group in every generation.	Branson's own adventures, and an irreverent, larky and sexy approach to marketing: always breaking the rules (a little).
	People who think business should be done by clean-shaven men in suits and ties.	Because the beard, jeans and jumper look makes Branson and his brands highly distinctive.	Uncompromising scruffiness on the part of Branson himself, with a balancing 'glamour' surrounding him.

Brand	Sample Enemy	Reason Why	Resulting Behaviour
	People who are so politically correct that they are offended by the sexism of Virgin's advertising.	Because in an increasingly politically correct cultural environment, the 'rock-star' chauvinism of Virgin is a cheerful, defiant antidote.	Overt glamour and apparently unreconstructed sexism of Virgin airline advertising.

EXERCISE 8: PLOTTING YOUR BRAND

Well, now, unsurprisingly, it's your turn. Using the table below, think hard about who your brand enemies are. If you're looking for a new job, who don't you want to work for? If you are planning to open a business, who are the customers that you don't want to attract? If you are seeking a new partner, what kind of person do you really not want to go on a date with, or even to spend the rest of your life with?

Brand	Sample Enemy	Reason Why	Resulting Behaviour

WHO DON'T YOU WANT TO APPEAL TO?

Brand	Sample Enemy	Reason Why	Resulting Behaviour

REAL-LIFE REINVENTORS ♥
Levi Roots: musician, chef and entrepreneur

As a young boy in Jamaica, Levi helped his grandmother in the kitchen. She taught him the secrets and subtleties of mixing Caribbean flavours, herbs and spices. Then, as an adult living in England, Levi recreated these amazing flavours in his own sauce, made from his kitchen in London's Brixton with the help of his seven children. He sold his popular Reggae Reggae Sauce out of a bag on his back at street festivals. After 16 years of rejection by banks and businesses that declined to invest in his sauce, Levi was spotted at the World Food Market by a BBC researcher and invited to take part in Dragon's Den, the TV show for would-be entrepreneurs. He won the investment needed to make the sauce, and a range of related products, a huge commercial success. Levi has also become a spokesperson for Caribbean cuisine, and entrepreneurship among the black community: 'I want to spread the word that if a black Brixtonian Rastafarian can make it with just a sauce, then you can make it too,' he says.

Chapter 8

USING YOUR IMAGINATION

As children we used our imaginations freely and powerfully. We could conjure up entire worlds of adventure while crawling under the dining room table or in a clump of trees. We could drop to all fours and become animals, or turn kitchen implements or any bound objects into the equipment of soldiers, astronauts or explorers. We were unabashed by the idea of pretending, and that ability to pretend gave us immense power and unbounded freedom.

Somehow, sadly, we seem to lose that sense of freedom as we enter adulthood. Sure, many of us will continue with imagination-based hobbies and fun activities, from online gaming to paintball. And we indulge our imaginations, to varying degrees, when we watch movies, read novels, follow a TV series and so on.

We also, it's true, continue to daydream, imagining ourselves with better lives – a little (or a lot) wealthier, enjoying exotic holidays or living in a nicer home in a better location. And more and more of us it seems are daydreaming about different ways of spending our days: better jobs, different careers, running our own businesses, retiring early, changing our lives...

Daydreaming is all very well. I'm sure it's healthy and I'm certain it's a key part of the process of change. I don't want to discourage anyone from daydreaming. On the contrary, I encourage you to create opportunities for daydreaming and to use them whenever they arise. You can't, by definition, control daydreaming but you can certainly give yourself more space for it to happen.

Those opportunities will be highly individual. I have a habit of letting myself doze for a few minutes after waking in the morning - against my actual inclination to leap out of bed and get on with work. The curious thing about what you might call enforced dozing is that, rather than going back to sleep, you seem to enter a semi-dream state, and from that state, countless insights into problems, and fresh solutions to new problems, seem to arise. My guess is that our brains are processing all this stuff of their own volition during the night. When we spring out of bed, without giving ourselves time to 'daydream', the ideas and inspirations are dutifully filed away by our obedient brains, which then get on with the demands of the day. If, on the other hand, you give yourself a few minutes of semi-awake dozing, then your brain may take the opportunity to present its overnight findings to you - like an enthusiastic office intern asking for a few minutes of your time to show you some 'off-the-wall ideas'.

Not all of my brain's overnight work is usable, of course, but some of my most creative, productive and positive thinking has sprung from these presentation sessions inside my head. They have influenced my writing, my brand advice activity, my other enterprises and my whole outlook on life. I am certain you have had the same experience many times; it's a part of the human condition. But, sadly, I think it has also become part of the modern human condition not to take these moments as seriously as we should. We seem to live in an ever-busier, ever more rational and process-driven world, in which the indulgence of reverie is faintly embarrassing to admit. My advice though, is simple: the reverie, the daydream, call it what you will, is one of our most powerful resources in moving forwards creatively.

Now that little homily might sound surprising coming from a hard-nosed marketing man. After all, I spend a great deal of my time trying to persuade would-be entrepreneurs to come back down to Earth, and I am a deep sceptic when it comes to the 'ask the universe and it shall be given' school of thinking. I am a rationalist, but I am also well aware of the power of the imagination to create possibilities. And it is possibilities that you need if you want to explore alternative futures.

BRAND NEW IMAGININGS

Commercial brand organizations explore new possibilities all the time.

How would it be if you made a new car with all the features and comforts that people expect in the

21st century, but which looked and felt like a 1960s classic car and conjured up *la dolce vita*? That little bit of imagination led to the fantastic success of the Fiat 500.

How would it be if you created a bookstore where you could buy virtually any book? Jeff Bezos had that little daydream and created Amazon.

How would it be if anyone (well, anyone seriously rich) could go into space? That ridiculous notion from Richard Branson is about to become reality. The first Virgin Galactic craft is under construction and hundreds of tickets have been pre-sold.

How would it be if you held a talent contest on TV which actually had the media power to create pop stars? The X Factor show and its many spin-offs have proved to be a hit with audiences all over the world.

How would it be if you created a device smaller than a laptop that was virtually a glass screen and could be used for web browsing, email, handling images and movies, games and all the usual laptop stuff such as writing and presentations? The iPad has changed the whole mobile technology marketplace, not to mention our expectations of what mobile devices can and should be for. In fact, I wrote this book on the device that sprang from imagining 'how would it be?' somewhere in Apple, and which many people said didn't have a *raison d'être*.

The point is, don't limit your imagination. I could list hundreds or thousands of examples but, more importantly, I want you to think of ways in which you can harness and exercise your imagination for the most powerful, positive effect on your personal, creative and/or working life.

Daydreaming is one way to achieve this. But the disadvantage of daydreaming is that its outputs all too easily slip away as soon as you return from reverie to full, in-the-world consciousness. So I have a few other methods that you might like to try in order to exercise your imagination in the kind of productive way we are looking for.

EXERCISE 9: EMAIL FROM THE FUTURE

The first is simply to write to yourself from an imagined future. I used to call this a letter from the future, but perhaps we should now call it an email from the future. A letter from the future is not a new or original idea, but it is a powerful one, and an email from the future is potentially even more powerful, because (as with emails in general) you can be rather more informal and iterative about it.

To start, pick a date at some imagined point in the future. There's no correct length of time into the future, but it's important to pick a time period that you can relate to in your imagination. If you're relatively young, a teenager perhaps, you might want to think just one or two years ahead, or even a matter of months. Then again you might be inclined to start imagining yourself a decade in the future, with a whole new adult life.

In my experience, a time gap of two to five years seems comfortable and effective – enough time to believe that you will have made some significant positive change in your life, but not so long that you won't recognize yourself. But it's your choice.

Once you've picked a time, the next step is fantastically simple, though quite thrilling, sometimes highly emotional, and rather profound.

Address an email to yourself and put your imagined future date in the subject line. Then simply start to write to yourself as though you (the writer from the future) are an old friend (of yours), and you're writing to say hello and to catch up.

Just let it flow. Write about your life and give it some detail. Where are you living – the same place or somewhere new? Alone or with someone? Do you have a family? What kind of work do you do? Are you affluent? What do you love to do in your free time? Perhaps it's something that you haven't even tried back in the present? Where do you go on holiday? Do you drive a car, or ride a motorbike or a bicycle? If so, what kind?

At this stage, in this first email, don't try to explain how you got to where you are now. After all it's the first contact for quite a long time, and you don't want to overwhelm your old self. So don't worry about the hows and whys, just concentrate on describing this future life.

Now sign off in a friendly way and press send.

And here's the fun part. Moments later you'll have an email drop into your inbox from a distant place: the future.

You don't have to read it straightaway. After all you only just wrote it. You can leave it there unread for an hour or two, or overnight. In fact, I'd recommend a slight delay because, when you do open it, it tends to seem somehow more real, more authentic.

I shouldn't really guarantee anything here, because I don't want you writing to me and telling me it didn't happen for you, but in this case I can pretty much promise you that reading this strange email in your inbox will be a peculiar and powerful experience.

It's not often that we actually allow ourselves the indulgence of imagining a future in detail, and that's what I meant by the idea of giving some robustness and discipline to the notion of daydreaming.

When you read the email, try to picture this old friend's life from what they've told you. Do they sound happy, fulfilled, excited? Have things worked out well for them?

Now it's time to write back and this is where, I hope, you'll see the point of restricting the first email to just describing life rather than how it came about. Now, in your reply, you get to ask the questions.

If the future you is living in some fantastically desirable location, in a wonderful home of some kind, do ask them how on Earth they managed to make that happen. How did they find it? And don't worry about being nosey (this is someone close to you after all). Ask them how they managed to afford such an amazing place. Don't worry, they won't be offended.

What about their work? It sounds like they have an amazing career, a dream job! Or they run their own business very successfully. Or maybe they've already sold a successful business and made a small, or large, fortune. Ask them to tell you how that happened. What was the secret of their success? What happened along the way? What were the key moments of success?

What were the challenges and difficulties they faced? How did they qualify for their fantastic job? How did they start their business?

What about their personal life? They've got fantastic friends and, best of all, a dream partner, maybe even kids. Ask them how they managed to make that catch.

And so on. Ask away. Be personal – you really need to learn from this person who seems to have achieved exactly what you would like, only even better.

Tell them how grateful you'll be for their reply, wish them well and sign off. Press send.

Of course, in real life, when you send a long email to someone you don't expect them to write back to you within moments. It is the same in this exercise. Give them a little time. Get on with other things and put your future friend out of your mind.

Of course they won't have gone from your mind at all. Instead they'll have gone into an unconscious processing part of your brain, along with the questions in your email.

You know what's coming next. Give it a day (at least one sleep) then sit down at your computer and open up this email full of questions. Blimey! Your cheeky friend from the past wants to know everything about how you achieved what you have. From your career through to how you found your partner! Still, that's not a problem. You were close in the past and you'd like to help out. So it's time to answer the questions.

This time, in answering the questions, it's important to really let your imagination flow, and to give real detail.

You'll find yourself improvising (fibbing, if you like) to complete the gaps in the story, and it will get richer and more detailed as you go on.

Your correspondence with the future you is now begun and, like all correspondence with friends, it will be more enjoyable and fulfilling if you keep it up: if you put sufficient effort and time into it to establish a natural rhythm. It might seem a little like playing a game of chess with yourself, but don't let that put you off. This could be one of the most profound imaginative games you have played since childhood because in these emails you will, in effect, be freeing yourself from present reality and opening yourself up to future potential.

Remember that I said that one of the four key building blocks of brand is compelling narrative? This exercise has a key role in creating that compelling narrative about you.

REAL-LIFE REINVENTORS ♀
Katie Piper: charity campaigner

Katie Piper earned her living in the beauty industry as a model and TV presenter. She was on course for a high-flying career before, in 2008, she was savagely disfigured after an ex-boyfriend conspired with a mate to throw industrial-strength sulphuric acid into her face. They were both jailed for life. One side of Katie's face was destroyed as far as the fat layer and she lost the sight in her left eye. Fearing for the future and in terrible pain in the days that followed the attack, Katie wrote a note to her parents saying 'kill me'. Over the following months her features were rebuilt and she endured more than 30 operations, showing extraordinary courage to overcome the physical and emotional damage wrought by the attack and find a new, positive way of living. Refusing to settle for what she calls 'a life of regret', she has set up an inspiring charity, The Katie Piper Foundation to help others to live with burns and scars. 'For me, beauty used to be about the best figure and looking the prettiest when I walked into a room. Now, I've realized that is only surface beauty. I feel more beautiful and confident by surrounding myself with people that believe in me and encourage me. Now when I feel down, I tell myself that I have loads going for me and I feel attractive,' she says.

Chapter 9

BRAND 'POSITIONING' AND CREATING YOUR UNIQUE PLACE TO STAND

Here's a one-sentence history of marketing. When modern marketing began, around the turn of the 20th century, it wasn't about finding customers so much as meeting the demand for products, and the trick was to show that your product had great features and unrivalled benefits – with reliable quality at a competitive price – but as the century progressed, the balance of power changed and the need was to woo customers with a distinctive offering that gave your product a different 'position' in the 'mind of the consumer', as marketers were inclined to say.

That idea of positioning, which was articulated, if not actually invented, by an American named Al Ries and his co-author Jack Trout, was a revolutionary concept, arriving as it did at the end of the great advertising era of the 1960s (the age portrayed rather glamorously in the TV series *Mad Men*). The idea of positioning was first aired in 1972, in a series of legendary articles in *Advertising Age* magazine, and subsequently in the book *Positioning: the battle for your mind*. Positioning remains a massive buzzword in the fields of marketing but it's a term that is often misunderstood.

WHY POSITIONING MATTERS TO YOU

The most important characteristic of the idea is that it is a relative concept, not an absolute one. A product or brand's 'position' refers to how it is perceived in the mind of the market, relative to competing products or brands. This notion of relativity in brand is what makes positioning a powerful tool. Anyone can use it, from the smallest company struggling to break through, to the individual who wants to get hired, promoted or noticed.

You probably know a version of the following joke, and forgive me for I am not a great joke teller. Two Arctic explorers are trudging across a snow-covered ice field. Suddenly they spot a huge, aggressive-looking polar bear less than half a kilometre away, and it is bounding towards them. One of the explorers sits down in the snow, pulls off his snowshoes and boots and retrieves from his backpack a pair of Nike running shoes, which he quickly laces up. The second explorer looks on in astonishment. 'Even in your Nikes you can't outrun a polar bear,' he says. 'I don't need to outrun it,' the first explorer replies.

And that, in a rather clunky way, is what positioning is about. You don't need to win anything absolutely.

You just need to win relative to the competition. And to do that you don't need to be 'better' than them. You just need to be different from them.

We humans have a staggering tendency to imitate each other. We dress similarly. We read (by definition) the same bestsellers. We watch (again by definition) the same hit TV shows. In general, we don't want to stand out from the crowd too much.

It's the same with companies and products – they have a remarkable tendency to flock around an idea.

I spend a lot of time in bookshops (reading, writing, drinking coffee and, occasionally, buying a book) and this tendency to flocking can be seen very markedly in popular fiction. The strong trends of the last couple of years include Scandinavian crime – which features numerous different authors who are all declared as the new Henning Mankell or Stieg Larsson – and dark fantasies of the vampire variety following the popularity of the *Twilight* series and the *True Blood* books.

But it's not just the themes of hit books that are imitated to the point of tedium (until everyone who wants to devour vampire romances has had their surfeit and is sated, so to speak), it is also the cover designs. Even, weirdly, the author's names seem to follow some kind of trend within each hit genre. It's the same in popular nonfiction too, from paperbacks that reveal the weirdness of the world through economics, statistics or other angles of view, through to the incredible success of books promising an insight into the application of the 'law of attraction'.

Imitating, or flocking as I call it, isn't necessarily a bad thing. If you're an author and you can jump aboard a trend while it's still got some life in it, then there are strong arguments in your favour. And if you're a company producing a product or service of any kind, from a coffee shop to a car manufacturer, then, if you time it right and can get to market quickly and efficiently, then following a trend has its merits.

However, and it's a big however, while imitation can give some short-term benefits (sales, if you're selling something), it won't help you to build a strong brand.

That's because (staying in the commercial world for a moment) joining the trendy pack can give you sales today, but only building a brand can give you sales tomorrow, and next year and next decade.

Sticking with the idea of popular fiction by way of example, if you write a novel about teenage love and angst, coupled with the idea that one or more of your characters is a vampire, or a werewolf, then all you can really be in a brand sense is 'the new Stephanie Meyer' or 'the best thing since *Twilight*'.

And to go back a few years (wow, it's amazing how fast these things move), if you wanted to write a book about a schoolboy learning to become a wizard, then the best you could hope to be is 'the new J.K. Rowling'. The reality of course is that publishers catch on pretty quickly to trends, milk them swiftly and efficiently and then move on. I dare you to try to get a schoolboy wizard book published any time before the end of this decade! The reason being that publishers aren't looking for the next *Harry Potter*, or the next *Twilight* – they are looking for the next thing that absolutely isn't *Harry Potter* or *Twilight* but which can enjoy similar success.

Creating a position

One way to think about 'positioning' is to imagine a huge wall-mounted storage system consisting of pigeonholes – the kind found in concierges in hotels or in shared office buildings for incoming mail. In our imaginary pigeonhole system there are infinite slots available and vast numbers of them are empty. Unclaimed you might say, and waiting for an occupant. But, hey, look at the one marked 'schoolboy wizards'. That one is full, with a pile of books by one author, not to mention DVDs of the movies based on the books. There are one or two books on similar themes stuffed in there as well, but it's blindingly obvious there's no room for anything else in the schoolboy wizards' slot. Now look at the slot marked 'teenage vampires'. That one is rammed full to bursting too, and some recent attempts to add more have failed (there's an untidy pile on the floor way beneath the slot).

So, if you want a publisher to pick up your next novel in the hope that it's the fantasy hit of the decade, you'd better make sure it fits in a pigeonhole that isn't already occupied. In other words, you need to find an empty 'position'.

The first truth about positioning then is that it is relative rather than absolute. 'Simply the best', is not a position for precisely that reason (and also, as I have told many clients, just plain lame). As an aside, if you ever get asked in an interview to explain why you should get the job, please don't say, 'because I'm the best'. That's not a position.

The second most important (and somewhat uncomfortable) truth about positioning is that it is very much a two-sided affair: as a brand, or an individual, you can 'claim' any position you think is appropriate, but because everything in branding depends on 'perception' (what the audience thinks and feels), your desired position is by no means guaranteed. There is a very real sense in which brand position has to be won, or earned. To add further challenge to the mix, the market itself is rarely, if ever, static. The book market, as we've seen, has moved on from schoolboy wizards and teenage vampires. The market shifts constantly in all kinds of unpredictable ways and what appears to be a rock-solid position today may seem like a very wobbly one tomorrow.

British Airways positioned itself for many years as 'The World's Favourite Airline'. This was based on the fact that it flew more people on more routes than anyone else, and interpreting that, somewhat wistfully, as meaning it was better liked than any other airline. In the past few years, however, BA has faced difficult times in a shifting marketplace and with all sorts of other issues threatening its claimed position.

Nevertheless, for all its challenges, the concept of positioning provides a hugely powerful lever for you in developing your personal brand, providing you choose a position that is genuinely available (an empty pigeonhole not already 'owned' by a competitor) and also authentic to you and credible to your audience. There really is nothing to be gained by taking a position that is distinctive and credible but puts your brand in such a refined place that nobody can relate to you.

Taking a position

But how do you choose a position? And how exactly do you do it effectively? There's no such thing as the right position, just positions that work and those that don't. We've already established the first rule of positioning: you can't take one taken by someone else, at least not within the same marketplace at the same time.

This puts me in mind of the legendary three-word pitch made to the studio to get backing for the pioneering movie *Alien*, directed by Ridley Scott. The movie was pitched simply as '*Jaws* in Space'. It's a neat piece of positioning because it gives a strong association with something that's already been successful, and gives a strong clue as to what its characteristic ingredients will be (tension, slow build-up, sudden horror, sustained fear). But it also places those elements in a fresh new context: Space. So *Alien* wasn't trying to fit into the *Jaws* pigeonhole (unlike another, less successful movie of the day, *Orca*, which might well have been pitched as 'a lame copy of *Jaws* but with a killer whale instead of a shark'.

And there's a powerful lesson in there for anyone wanting to create a brand positioning for themselves: be *Jaws* or *Alien*, not *Orca*.

Let's move on from popular fiction and movies, and think about some well-known brands in other fields to illustrate just a few of the possible ways to approach positioning.

- You can take a position based on a product's attributes: such as Guinness, which makes an epic virtue of the time it takes for a pint of the black stuff to settle.

- You can take a position based on occasions when a product is used, such as Kit Kat's strong association with taking a well-earned 'break'.

- You can take a position according to the aspirations of your customer, such as Coutts, which is firmly identified as the Queen's bank.

- You can take a position based on your values: the Co-operative Bank has strongly associated itself with ethical finance.

- You can take a position based on a 'promise', such as John Lewis's 'Never Knowingly Undersold', or FedEx's commitment to getting your package to its destination overnight.

- You can take a position alongside other brands or a whole category, such as Intel's brilliant 'Intel Inside' campaign, which has given a hidden component the status of a customer-facing brand.

- You can take a position against other brands. Perhaps the most famous example is the car-hire company Avis, which, since 1962, has consistently claimed 'We try harder' (originally to distinguish itself from the market leader, Hertz).

- You can take a position against a whole category: such as Apple's 'I'm a Mac' campaign, which starkly contrasted the Apple ethos against the rest of the PC industry.

PUTTING IT ALL TOGETHER

That's all very well for businesses and products, but if you're an individual how do you apply the same logic? Well, like many of the concepts in this book, it requires something of a leap of faith. Not because it's difficult but because it's actually simple.

Imagine you're in the hypothetical interview scenario again. One of the things interviewees are usually asked to do is to describe 'what they will bring to the company' (or words to that effect). This is where a considered position (and by that I mean considered in advance not improvised on the spur of the moment) can be so effective.

The first thing you MUST NOT DO is say that you don't really know, or even that you're 'not sure, but...'

The second thing you MUST NOT DO is to try to claim something absolute, some all-encompassing quality that indicates you are in some way or other 'simply the best'.

Hopefully the reason for not committing the first sin is obvious (er... don't go to any interview that unprepared). But the reason for not committing the second is to do with positioning. As we've said, 'the best' is not a position, so the only thing interviewers learn from that claim is that you are self-confident, or more likely that you are compensating for a lack of genuine self-confidence.

Better, I would suggest, is to say something like: 'I am utterly reliable and I learn by asking intelligent questions and listening to the answers.'

Or perhaps: 'All the training and experience of my career to date has given me exactly the right set of skills for this role, and I always make sure I am completely up-to-date with the latest developments in the field.'

Or, simply: 'I am more helpful with customers because I've taken the trouble to observe customer service in shops, restaurants and elsewhere and I know exactly what most people get wrong when it comes to making customers feel important.'

So the first example is about reliability and constant improvement. The second is about diligence and commitment, and the third is about service.

These answers aren't just vague claims. They are quite specific in that they have a little detail attached and offer some evidence. In so doing they avoid the 'simply the best' trap. They aren't boastful, but they are clear. They don't have the snap of 'The World's Favourite Airline', but then you're not an airline, you're a person.

EXERCISE 10: CREATING A POSITION

This exercise invites you to create a 'position' for yourself. In order to do that you need to think of your context. Is it work, romance or business, or are you trying to get a job? It's important to think about this because a position is, as we've established, a relative thing, and your position may well vary according to the situation (the market) in which you are operating.

Start by deciding what 'market' you want to apply your thinking to initially. You can move on to others later. Write it down as a header ('interview', 'looking for pay rise', 'social group', 'dating', for example). Then under the header I want you to think about your authentic strengths.

A list for a job interview might look like this:

- *Reliable*

- *Fast learner*

- *Friendly*

- *Good with detail*

- *Qualified*

- *Appropriate previous experience*

Now these are all good things, but there are too many of them to constitute a distinctive position. Choose one or two and focus on them. And my advice is, always choose the most distinctive ones (which is to say a pigeonhole that is unlikely to be occupied). You don't have to claim to be 'friendly', for example. Everybody claims that. Instead, just 'be' friendly. And there's nothing terribly interesting about claiming that you're 'qualified' and have 'appropriate experience' because that is evidenced on your CV and you probably wouldn't be in the interview room otherwise. That leaves you with being reliable, a fast learner and good with detail. You're starting to get a position here. You can refine it further, of course, but I'd say that being utterly reliable (a reassuring promise when so many people aren't), being a fast

learner and paying attention to detail (if that's what
the job requires) is a pretty strong position to take.
Now it's your turn.

A few years ago, when I started my own consultancy,
I really didn't have a 'position'. I was quite good at
creative thinking and solving problems. I knew about
branding. I was quite a good speaker. Plus, I had done
a bit of writing. But to all audiences, beyond those
who already knew me, I was just another ex-agency
guy offering a mixed bag of consultancy. Then, as
I've recounted elsewhere, I changed my brand. More
importantly, I changed my position. Instead of the
vague and not very compelling description that I've just
given, I positioned myself as 'a strategic brand expert
who can make the power of branding understandable
and accessible to help you make profound changes
to your company or organization'. I called this Brand
Strategy Guru but it was the position that was critical.

Subsequently, I've moved to being 'a brand expert
author, speaker and adviser', which is more succinct
and provides more 'evidence'. Positions can, and must,
change as you and your circumstances change.

Now and again – and maybe for you it is now –
there is a need to do what is known as 'repositioning'.
When you reposition you go through a process of
dismantling current perceptions about you, and
creating new ones.

So thinking about your positioning is not just about
making a career move, it can actually change the way
you think about yourself, boosting your confidence
and your determination.

REAL-LIFE REINVENTORS ♀

Alain Coumont: founder of Le Pain Quotidien organic
bakeries, cafes and food shops

Alain Coumont is the son and grandson of grocers. As a child
he spent hours perched on a chair, watching his grandmother
make bread. Then, in 1977, inspired by one of the founders
of nouvelle cuisine, chef Michel Guérard, he enrolled at
hotel school. After graduating he worked in a number of
top-flight restaurants. As a young chef in Brussels, Alain
couldn't find the right bread for his restaurant. Passionate
about quality, he returned to his roots and opened a small
bakery where he could knead flour, salt and water into
the rustic loaves he remembered from his childhood. He
opened his bakery in an avant-garde area of Brussels in
1990 and named it Le Pain Quotidien. The city quickly took
to the taste of this traditional bread and Alain evolved his
offerings to include simple salads and tartines, keeping
bread as the cornerstone of his small menu. At a local flea
market, he found a long table where his guests could sit to
eat together; it became Le Pain Quotidien's first communal
table and helped create his signature simple, rustic style,
which has flourished to become an international business.

Chapter 10

CRAFTING YOUR BRAND STORY: PAST, PRESENT AND FUTURE

In the world of brands and branding, story is king! Narrative rocks and rules. If all other elements of a brand equation are equal, then the best brand story will always win the day. In other words, if you have two identical products sitting on the shelf next to each other - cornflakes or DVD players, it doesn't matter - and they are both the same price, of the same design, from the same country of origin and in every other way a perfect substitute for each other, then which one are you going to buy? It's blindingly obvious - you will always (always) pick the one with the name that you recognize: the brand that you trust. In fact, if you've heard of one and not the other, you don't even have to trust it (you might know nothing about it but its name). You will still pick that one, but the question is, 'Why?'

The reason is hard-wired into our humanity. We are pattern-making creatures. We are constantly trying, consciously and unconsciously, to make patterns from the world around us. And we do this because the alternative is not only impractical but also hugely stressful. Unless we make patterns, every experience and encounter will be a new one. Now that might make life interesting, but it would also, of course, make life unbearable and dangerous.

We are not alone. All animals learn to respond to particular stimuli - it's a survival mechanism. But in humans it has become something more: a way to make sense of the world. From coping with the primitive fear that the sun will set and fall to rise again, to decisions about whom we can trust in business, we make patterns in order to avoid having to work everything out afresh every day and every hour.

And in making our patterns, we are uniquely given to the creation of stories - narratives that we can pass on to each other, down the generations, or across the social group, to explain and establish these learned patterns in the minds and hearts of others. And other humans are doing the same to and for us. This is, in a sense, a definition of culture.

In the 21st century, pattern-making and its associated narrative-making have reached a kind of zenith. We now live and function (with varying degrees of success, happiness and health) in a staggeringly 'branded' world. But why should brands have become such a phenomenon? How have we allowed them to become such a powerful influence on our behaviour? It is because branding is really storytelling. Brands are not just an economic phenomenon, but also a cultural one. We use brands (and I'm not saying this is a good, bad or indifferent fact, just that it's a fact) as part of the narrative fabric of our modern world.

Branding, therefore, isn't just a technique used by marketers to influence us (although it certainly does that), it has become part of the cultural language we use to speak to each other, and indeed ourselves, about our interests, our aspirations, our passions and the very definition of who we are and how we see our place in the world.

Again, I should stress that I am not celebrating this fact. Nor am I decrying it. But we do need to face up to it because it plays a huge role in influencing our decisions about what we need to do if we want to change the definition of ourselves and our place in the world.

In other words, if we accept that brand is about stories and their interpretation, and we also acknowledge that brands have an immensely powerful influence on what we buy (or support, or become members of, or vote for), we have to draw the conclusion that narrative, which is about creating meaning, is a hugely powerful influence on human behaviour.

And from that point, we must conclude that this applies to interactions way beyond shopping. It also applies when we are considering potential dating partners, or interview candidates, or business suppliers, or employees asking for promotion or a raise.

TELLING YOUR STORY

Your story is arguably one of your strongest weapons. Others might argue that reputation really deserves that title, but reputation is actually a form of story. In the end it all comes back to story.

Let's think a little about what that concept of story really means. It certainly doesn't mean something that you (or a company) makes up. I'm not talking about fantasy, exaggeration, fibs or spin, because all those things are fragile constructions that might fool some of the people some of the time, but will ultimately be uncovered and brought down. The truth will out eventually. If you make a bad product but tell false stories about its efficacy and quality, you will probably flog some stuff for a while. You may even get rich, but sooner or later phoney stories have a wonderful habit of collapsing around the ears of the teller.

So, for our purposes story isn't about inventing things but about channelling truths to create a coherent, integrated, holistic narrative that has emotional, as well as intellectual, impact on those to whom you tell it, and on yourself.

At the beginning of this chapter I discussed product choices in order to illustrate the importance of branding in the commercial world – the 'shopping' world. But really we are not talking about product choices. We are talking about people choices.

You might, legitimately, be wondering how on Earth you can create such a story for yourself: how you tell a story that can, in effect, become a brand narrative powerful enough to engage your target audience. Well, the trick, I believe, is to think of the process not as creating a story, but as uncovering a story. Your story already exists: what you have to do is reveal it (first to yourself) and then to shape it.

A lot of us make two mistakes when we think about our life stories (and I'm not including the outrageously self-confident people who think they are the most interesting people on the planet – I'm thinking of the rest of us). The first mistake is to think that our story is not interesting, let alone compelling. The second is to think that it is too disparate and messy to be considered a story at all.

We are so close to our own lives that it is sometimes terribly difficult or even impossible to step back far enough to see the pattern: the exciting and meaningful narrative. Yet it's there. It's always there. I promise.

Over a long time of considering this aspect of brand, and how brand can be applied to individual life stories, I have come to use a particular metaphor to try to visualize this idea of the drawing together of different elements of a life to create a powerful narrative.

Picture a tree. You're looking at a huge mature tree, an oak maybe. But the difference is that you see what's below ground, as well as above. So you can clearly see not just the immensely strong trunk, the great boughs that reach out from it, the smaller branches that eventually become tiny twigs, and their leaves, but also (because we're picturing it in our mind's eye) the roots below the ground. You're surprised, nay amazed, to see that the roots and their millions of tendrils present a kind of reflection of the growth of the branches above. The roots reach deep into the soil and draw the vital moisture and nutrients that give the tree life.

OK, enough of the heroic potential of tree imagery for a moment. Just see the tree as a metaphor for a life story - your life story. The roots are not only representative of your home, your childhood and your background, but also of the threads of early ambition, dreaming, fantasy and personal development that happen in infancy, childhood and youth.

The trouble, for many of us, is that we have a strong tendency in adulthood to forget (to leave hidden below the ground as it were) all those magical elements, and to think that now, as adults with all our adult struggles, we must concentrate on the here and now and the adult world.

The trunk of the tree is your strength in the present. It is you, now, solid and real. And it can also, like a tree, be fixed and unbending. The tree cannot move. It can only develop by growing its branches and leaves, by stretching out a little and reaching constantly. And to allow and support that stretching and reaching, it has to draw constantly on the hidden strength below ground: the roots. In fact, it is has not only to draw on the strength of the roots, but also to nourish and grow them - going ever deeper and wider to provide stability.

So there are three vital elements in this tree metaphor. The roots - your roots - provide you with strength and stability, but they need to be constantly nourished and fed. The trunk - your presence in the world now - draws on the roots but is also unable to move and grow unless it continually reaches outwards and upwards. The branch system - your ambition and growth - is only possible because of the strength of the trunk and the integrity of the roots. And throughout the whole, from the tips of the tiniest roots to the highest leaves at the end of the longest branches, flows the stories that make up your life. And all of them, from the trivial to the tragic, have the potential to be incredibly important in fashioning your narrative.

I hope you don't find this metaphorical approach too far-fetched. I'm a grounded and businesslike kind of guy, but sometimes only a metaphor will do.

EXERCISE 11: FINDING YOUR NARRATIVE THREADS

Now I want you to use this tree metaphor in an exercise. There are three simple stages to this exercise.

The linear description

First, I want you to take your life story and express it in a linear way, as a series of bullet points, and as much in chronological order as you can make it. Don't use your imagination in this first part of the exercise, just use your memory. And include everything. Include the stuff you wanted to do, as well as the stuff you did, and the stuff you do now. Include the things you love and the things you hate. The things that make you feel fulfilled and the things that make you feel worthless. Include all the little triumphs and the disasters.

Your list can be any length. It doesn't matter. If you're young you might fill it with more detail because you might include school and college experiences. You can add as much or as little detail as you like. The point is to get it all down as non-judgementally as possible.

Here's what an edited version of my list looks like.

- *Wanna-be racing driver, poet, short-story writer*
- *Student teacher*
- *Junior PR*
- *Business journalist*
- *Student nurse*
- *Staff nurse*
- *Training manager in the NHS*
- *Struggling freelance writer*
- *Ad agency creative director*
- *Brand strategy consultant*
- *Author of business books*
- *Conference speaker*

Now it's your turn...

Finding the threads

Now we come to the second and really exciting part of this exercise: finding the threads that run through your list, from root tip to branch and leaf. They are there, even if you find it hard to see or acknowledge them. I want you to look at the list until you find your threads.

At this stage you are looking for the powerful themes, which you can draw on, that give you strength of character and make you unique, but which you also need to nurture in order to be all that you can be.

Some of those threads will be skills and personality traits, while others might be achievements. It doesn't matter whether they are humble or grand. This isn't a competition. The important thing is to create a powerful set of elements for your personal brand narrative.

It is impossible, of course, to pre-judge what your collection of narrative threads might look like. My confident prediction, though, is that by looking for these threads, you will find a power in your life story and your potential future that you may not have realized was there before.

Here's a few of mine, just to give you the idea.

- *Writing: I've always written (bad) poetry and (quite bad) short stories. I have written professionally over many years, as a copywriter, creative director and now an author.*

- *Entrepreneurship: I'm not a successful entrepreneur. I haven't made my million. But I have started small businesses that have survived and thrived and I've learned something about what to do and what not to do.*

- *Performing and communicating: it's the desire and ability to show off, which arrived late in my life, that allows me to sing in public (although I know my talent is limited) and to stand up and speak about brands and marketing in front of conference audiences.*

When you look at your first list it might seem (as mine certainly did to me) a little messy, confusing and incoherent but in the second part of the exercise you'll start to see all the disparate elements through different eyes. When you look at the 'threads' that run through your life story, things can start to make more sense.

Drawing it all together

The third part of the process is simple: it is just to consider those threads and to contemplate how they might inform the reinvention of yourself – 're-branding' You.

This process enabled me to understand clearly that I needed to combine my writing and my desire to communicate with my entrepreneurial spirit to 'position' myself. It's this process that has enabled me to be what I am now.

Now I want you to do the same contemplation. Consider the threads. What do they tell you about your true potential? Is it possible that you have been ignoring your obvious talents and personality traits, as so many of us do for so long?

Contemplate the threads and imagine how drawing them together can give you a new position, a new story, even a new destiny.

I hope this exercise will give you some powerful raw material. In the next chapter we will look at shaping that material into a story which is powerful, punchy and compelling to those you need to engage beyond yourself.

REAL-LIFE REINVENTORS ▼
Fraser Doherty: jam-maker and entrepreneur

Fraser Doherty is the self-proclaimed 'jam boy' who now runs a multi-million-pound jam-making business thanks to a strong personal story that has fuelled his success in life. When he was 14, his grandmother Susan wracked her brains about how to keep him occupied one afternoon. She decided to show him how to make her secret jam recipe and Fraser loved what they produced together. The first few jars were sold to neighbours, then further along the street. He made more and sold them at a local church fête. They were an incredible success. Soon he was producing 1,000 jars a week from his parents' kitchen. Customers loved his delicious jam, which relied on his gran's secret recipe to make the healthiest possible product. Before long, the popular product was made commercially and is now called SuperJam. It sells into major supermarket chains and Fraser now produces more than 500,000 jars every year.

Chapter 11
HOW TO *TELL* YOUR BRAND STORY

In the last chapter we looked at the importance of storytelling in building your brand. It works in the commercial world and with individuals, too. Those who tell the best stories make the most impact: they win the promotion, secure the job, get the pay rise, get the date and so on.

But note, the important verb in that sentence is 'tell'. It's not enough just to have a great story. You have to find a way to tell it, too.

It's not difficult but, like all the other elements of building your brand, it requires a little thought.

Above everything else (and this will be unpopular with some people for the same reasons that anything to do with the so-called dark arts of marketing and branding are unpopular) I believe the first person you have to think about when you think of how to tell your story is not actually you. No, the person you need to think about is your listener, your audience. You may find this an uncomfortable thought. And it is likely to be an unpopular notion with anyone who is of the mindset that they must express their unique individuality and personality at all costs.

We are getting into difficult territory here, because I am not asking you to conform, or to be just like all the others – far from it actually. I absolutely want you to stand out from the crowd, but with a specific purpose in mind: and that purpose is not fundamentally about 'self-expression' in the normal sense of the term.

Frankly, to express yourself you don't need the help of this or any other book. You can just 'be' and 'do' exactly as you feel. My late father was a keen amateur painter. He had some talent, but not heaps. And he loved to paint. He painted with passion and vigour and with a total and delightful disregard for the taste or interest of others. He was a true 'self-expressionist' and I admired and respected him for it. He also never sold a single picture. But it wasn't limited talent that prevented him from selling. It was his determination to paint exactly as he chose. He cheerily scorned those whom he referred to as the 'Sunday painters', despite the fact that he was a Sunday painter, too. What differed was his attitude and his intent. He was a hobbyist but he pursued his hobby as though it was true artistic endeavour – self-expression pure and simple, and hugely admirable.

Self-expression is a vital and thrilling part of our human nature. But self-expression is not about telling your story primarily to others, but about telling a story about yourself, to yourself. And that's not what concerns us. In fact, counter-intuitive and uncomfortable though it may feel, the truth is that when you are creating a personal brand you have to sublimate the need to express yourself into something more important, which is to present a compelling story that will engage others.

To put it another way, you want 'you' to stand out from the crowd in whatever context you need to, by clearly being the exceptional candidate in terms of your quality, but not in terms of you making a superficial 'novelty' impact, or indeed by being seen (or more likely ignored or invisible) because you are so concerned with self-expression that you are blind to the interests of others.

In fact, I urge you to be the most 'appropriate' you can be to the circumstances. Again, I have to stress, I don't mean be the same as the others. I mean be the one who clearly stands out as 'best in class' for the prospective new employer, raise-giver, potential date or even life partner, and so on.

And you don't get to be best in class by being loyal to self-expression above all else, but by responding with your individuality to what your listener/audience wants.

There's a truism about marketing as a discipline that is profound yet frequently neglected by marketers. It is that marketing is not the art of selling more of the product or service that you provide. That's not marketing at all: that's selling. Rather, marketing is fundamentally about understanding what the customer wants or needs, or could possibly want or need in the future, and responding appropriately.

When you think about your brand narrative, think like a marketer: the customer comes first, your need for self-expression should only ever be second. This book is not only about you finding who you really are, and what you really want, but also about taking that 'brand new you' out into the world.

YOUR BRAND NARRATIVE

By now, you should have a kind of story tree: a number of different elements about you, your character, your skills and your achievements (no matter how small they seem to you) which together form something that is distinctly you. But you can't just take that bundle of story elements and dump them on another person in the hope they will be mightily impressed. Well, of course you can do that, but I don't think (unless you are exceptionally gifted, staggeringly charming, or unfeasibly lucky) that this tactic is going to achieve the optimum result.

Instead you need to shape your little bundle of story possibilities to suit your audience.

Sometimes in branding we think about all the different potential elements of a brand story as the control knobs on a fancy guitar amplifier. You know the old *Spinal Tap* gag, with the guitarist who is so devoted to playing loud that his amplifier knobs go up to 11? Of course you do.

Well, turning everything up to 11 is precisely NOT what we want to achieve. What we want to do is adjust the different knobs representing each of the elements of your story depending on your specific audience.

So in my case, I regularly turn the dial up on some things and down on others, depending on the circumstances. My corporate branding clients aren't much interested that I have another life singing in a band, so I mention it only at the foot of my CV or biography. It gets a tiny mention because it adds a little bit of flavour to the business stuff, but that's all.

Music promoters and music magazines, on the other hand, don't need to know that I make my living by talking about business and marketing. In fact, it can make me look less credible as a musician, which may be unfair and illogical but that's life. I therefore turn the business dial way down (almost to zero). I say almost but not completely, because, when dealing with promoters, agents and so on, a certain amount of business savvy and professionalism is appreciated. At least they know you're going to turn up to play.

Similarly, on Left Hand Bear I tend to dial up my music credentials, but as supporting my passion for providing a service to other musicians, rather than my 'corporate' story, because that is of direct relevance and interest to my customers.

These days the dials are being adjusted again, because I am more often speaking to general audiences rather than purely business audiences. Now my music thread is more relevant, because it is part of the whole story about developing a personal brand.

So on my corporate Brand Strategy Guru website (brandstrategyguru.com) my musical life barely gets a mention, but on my author/speaker site (www.simon middleton.com) music gets a whole page. Different audiences, different emphasis. See the difference?

So, the first principle in telling your brand story is to dial up or dial down the various elements, depending on your audience.

EXERCISE 12: DIALLING UP, DIALLING DOWN

Draw some simple dials/knobs for yourself and label each with an element of your story. Then think about which elements you will dial up or down in different circumstances. Draw the numbers 1 to 11 on each to help bring the whole concept to life.

The elements for each circumstance will be the same, but then of course, you have to choose your audience for each set. One set of dials might be aimed at a 'new employer' if you are looking for a job. Another set of dials might be aimed at your ideal date or partner. This will depend entirely on your circumstances and your ambitions. You may have a couple of audiences, or you may have a dozen, depending on the complexity of your life. You may want to concentrate on just one target audience and that's fine, too.

The important thing is to think about what elements are most likely to gain a positive response from that audience (which can, of course, be an individual person).

RESPECT AND LOVE

The popular branding concept of 'Lovemarks' (created by Kevin Roberts and explained in his superb books *Lovemarks* and *The Lovemarks Effect*) states that brands of any kind have only two elements with which they can work: respect and love.

Respect refers to the rational engagement with a product, service or company. It's about what we think about something. We think this product is a reasonable price. We think this service will do what we need. We think this company is fairly reliable. On the other hand, love refers to our emotions. It's not about what we think but about what we feel. Some brands manage to get us to actually feel something for them. In some cases they get us to fall in love with them to the point where we champion their virtues to others and defend them against criticism.

For Kevin Roberts (and I couldn't agree more) the magic really starts when respect (rational) is combined with love (emotional). When these two elements are both in play, says Roberts, we have a new brand phenomenon, which he calls the 'Lovemark'. 'Lovemarks' are able to command great customer loyalty, to charge higher prices, to more easily fend off competition, and to ask and receive forgiveness when they get things wrong.

There are many things to learn from the 'Lovemarks' concept, but the most pertinent one here is that when we tell our brand stories (and it is plural rather than singular because we have, as explained above, various versions of the story which we use with different audiences), we can use these magic elements of respect and love, too.

A story that is all about the rational (a respect story) runs the risk of being boring. Facts, data and information are important but they can be dull, too.

We've all met people who are so keen to tell us every factual component of a story that they end up boring us half to death (and most of us have been guilty of doing it ourselves at some point in our lives, too).

On the other hand, when it is unsupported by thought, emotion (whether upbeat or downbeat) can be equally problematic. Brands that appeal only to our emotions in an attempt to make us love them can be quite quickly off-putting. And that's not just to do with sentimentality. Overuse of humour, or simple over-enthusiasm, can be very wearing, in people as well as in brands.

You only have to think about TV commercials that you see daily to understand how most brands fall into the trap of being either too 'rational' or too 'emotional'.

Laptop computer advertising is virtually always over-burdened with factual information. The advertisers tell us about memory capacity, processor speed and other technical features, and then give us the ultimate rational bit of information: low price! It's a soulless approach to advertising. That's not to say that it doesn't sell products. Of course it does. But it doesn't build brand. And by focusing exclusively on selling products now and neglecting the building of brand, such advertising has a short-term effect.

By way of dramatic contrast, think of the perfume advertising that you see throughout the year but most often in the run-up to gift-giving holidays such as Christmas. Perfume commercials are very light on information (there really isn't much information to give, after all) but very heavy on emotion. Specifically, perfume commercials tend to focus on emotional responses relating to beauty, mystery, sensuality and, of course, sex. This kind of advertising clearly has strength for the perfume sector (otherwise they wouldn't keep doing it), but most of us are (despite having our emotional buttons involuntarily pressed, so to speak) also somewhat cynical about the grandiosity and pretentiousness of this approach. We know we are being emotionally manipulated.

So if too much rationality and too much emotion leave us feeling unsatisfied, how do we tell a story that gets the balance right? The simple answer is by being aware of the balance. By paying attention to the rational/emotional mix of your narrative, you will give yourself an edge over most people who are attempting to communicate something about themselves.

In other words, you can immensely improve the effectiveness of the way you tell your brand story (or stories) by pausing to think about the balance between the rational and the emotional (respect and love).

EXERCISE 13: FINDING YOUR HEAD AND HEART

With that thought in mind, it's time to take your brand narrative, as you developed it in the previous chapter, and look at it again through the lens of emotion and rationality.

The simplest way to do this is to put the elements of your story under two headings. Let's just call them 'Head' and 'Heart'. Remember to include things that have a sensory effect (beauty and desirability for example) under Heart (emotion).

By way of illustration, let's assume you are a devastatingly attractive theoretical physicist with tremendous DIY skills and a fantastically well-paid job that you love and do with ease, leaving you time and energy to pursue your passion for charitable works.

Lucky you: you've got big ticks under both the Head and the Heart headings. You're quite a catch (for the right kind of person). In fact, your problem may be in managing your story so you don't sound too 'perfect' – nobody likes a show-off after all.

For most of us, though, the more likely outcome of creating a double column list like this is that one side or the other is likely to have the greater number of ticks. Our brand narrative is likely to be stronger in either Head or Heart, rather than equally balanced.

In order to build a strong personal brand, which will serve you well over time and in different circumstances, you need some kind of balance. You need to appeal to the emotional and the rational.

This is true regardless of your audience. In applying for a job, for example, it would be very easy to assume that your rational/head assets (your qualifications, your experience, your skills) are more important. Counter-intuitive though it may seem, however, employers are increasingly inclined to hire people whose personalities will fit with their business (an emotional choice, in other words) over and above the more rational factors.

There is no such thing as perfect balance. Then, there is no such thing as an ideal brand story, any more than there is an ideal human being. Of course not. But achieving some kind of balance between the emotional and the rational will help to give your personal brand story a robust appeal, which a wildly imbalanced approach will not have.

TONE OF VOICE

We have looked at the head/heart balance and the notion of dialling up or down particular elements of your story depending on your audience and circumstances. The final point of this chapter concerns what marketing people tend to call 'tone of voice'.

Tone of voice refers both to the words you choose to use and the way that you use them. There is no tone of voice that is definitively right or wrong, of course. But there is, once again, a balance to be struck. In this case I believe that the balance is to be found somewhere between your unique 'self-expressive' voice and the voice of your particular audience.

Think about our hypothetical theoretical physicist again for a moment. If that physicist is as wise as she is clever, then she will carefully adjust the 'tone of voice' that she uses according to her audience. Not to do so will mean she will not be understood by anyone other than other theoretical physicists.

Of course she won't feign ignorance of her subject, or 'dumb down' her way of speaking, but she will find balance. Communication, after all, depends on some kind of equilibrium between the parties involved. You can't have real communication without it. Instead you have one party talking and the other simply (or more likely simply not) listening.

Commercial brands strive constantly to find an appropriate tone of voice to aid their communication. Most of them, frankly, struggle to find one that sounds authentic to them, yet is genuinely communicative to their audience. The best approach I believe is to aim for 'ordinary human'. Like so many suggestions in this chapter, aiming for ordinary might seem counter-intuitive or downright weird. But the benefits of ordinariness should not be underestimated when it comes to communication

Communicating 'usually' implies, by definition, that you are not using language that will bypass others or alienate them. And it implies that you have regard for the needs of your audience. Perhaps, most importantly, it demonstrates that you are not trying too hard, not overdoing it, not showing off, and that you are at ease with yourself and with the person or people with whom you are communicating. By being at ease, you put your audience at ease. You become, in effect, a brand to which they can relate.

REAL-LIFE REINVENTORS ⚲
Felix Finkbeiner: young environmentalist

At the age of nine, Felix Finkbeiner hatched an innovative plan to plant a million trees in Germany as part of a school project. Inspired by the work of Kenyan environmentalist Wangari Maathai, who organized the planting of 30 million trees, Felix gave a presentation to classmates at his Munich school. It was rapturously received. Two days later, his teacher encouraged him to give the same speech at the school council and shortly after for the head teacher. Soon he was talking to other classes. Two months after his initial speech, Felix launched the campaign in earnest by planting a crab apple tree in March 2007. News reached other schools, then the media and then the rest of the world and he set up an organization called Plant for the Planet. His first goal has already been achieved in Germany. The campaign is now spreading around the world, with the even more ambitious aim of planting a million trees in every country opting to take part. The ultimate goal is to plant 212 million trees across the globe. Supporters either donate money to buy a tree or head out and plant one. As a teenager, Felix, was named one of the most influential green activists in the world.

Chapter 12

BRINGING YOUR PERSONAL BRAND TO LIFE VISUALLY

Don't panic (I'm trying not to): this is not about colouring you beautiful or telling you to smarten up a bit. I am neither qualified to discuss fashion nor particularly interested in it.

So with those thoughts in mind, be reassured that I am not going to try to tell anyone how they should dress. That's not for me to say. Even if I was knowledgeable about things sartorial, there are simply too many variables to allow me, or I would suggest, anyone else, to give definitive advice.

What I do want to offer is perhaps an even greater challenge, which is to think about your visual appearance from the point of view of someone else.

But, you protest, don't we all do that anyway? Don't husbands seek reassurance from their wives? Don't friends seek admiration and reassurance from each other when they're getting ready to go out? And vice versa? Yes, of course, all this is true, but the nature of those enquiries is different from what I'm asking you to do.

For a start, the conventional question, 'Do I look alright in this?' is designed to elicit a positive answer. It's a question that doesn't really seek information, just confirmation. And of course the question is also, generally, referring to a fairly closed or limited social group and set of social norms. When asking the question, we are not usually about to step into a world that is markedly different to our own. Or so we might think.

In fact, we almost always (unless we make a special effort in particular circumstances) look at the world through our own preconceptions. Not really seeking to understand the views of others, just doing enough to get by.

To give an example: I began my working life in the early 1980s and at that time I thought it was more important to express my individuality than to 'fit in'. I was a rebel of sorts, which manifested in the clothes I wore – an odd mixture of cheap suits and a mod-style parka complete with badges.

Now in many contexts my scruffiness really wouldn't have mattered, but I worked for a PR company. I was pretty good at my job and survived, but my clothes undoubtedly had a negative impact on my career prospects. It was not because my clothing spoke so much about my personality but spoke much more loudly and accurately about my attitude to the company, my bosses, and the all-important clients. In short, my clothing choices reflected the fact that I hadn't yet come to terms with the transition from student-intellectual-rebel to someone with career ambitions. I was anti-establishment in my outlook yet I wanted to function in an establishment world. Difficult trick to pull off and the biggest obstacle to success was my choice of clothing.

I think I knew subconsciously that I had put a barrier between my employers, the clients and myself, but I was doing it accidentally and without regard for its effect on my prospects.

This story tells a deep truth about branding: all products, services, companies, organizations and people create and shape their brands all the time, but most of the time they do it without intent – by accident in other words.

FINDING YOUR BRAND STYLE

In the end, of course, we will all do as we wish. And I'm not suggesting there is a right or wrong way to dress, or a right or wrong personal brand to create. But I do suggest that the way you dress is one of the tools at your disposal and that it is also, by definition, one of the most visible aspects of your 'brand'. In short, it matters.

So how do you decide what clothing will enhance your brand, as opposed to detracting from it? I think there are three elements to consider.

To find the first element you have to go back to your overall strategic intent. You have to ask yourself what kind of brand you actually, consciously, determinedly want to create. You might want to go back to chapters 3 and 4 and look at the notes you made. This is critical because out of that strategic intent comes one key part of the answer to the question of what to wear.

If your strategic intent is to be an outsider in some way then the rest of your answer will fall into place in one particular way. And if your intent is to develop a career, or to win a partner, or a promotion, or for your consultancy business to win a client, then the answer will fall another way.

But until you have the other two elements in place, you still won't be clear.

So the second element – this is the one most usually neglected, and the place where I started this chapter – relates to the world-view of the people with whom you are trying to communicate.

You have to ask yourself: who are those people, how do they see the world, what do they need and want from me, and how do my choices about clothing and style influence them to form a view about me?

The third element is to explore and feel confident about finding a visual style or approach to dress and self-presentation that sits comfortably (in every sense) with your body, your personality and your lifestyle in a practical way.

It's a kind of Venn diagram of interlocking elements: your overall strategy, the viewpoint/mindset of your audience and your 'self'.

Figure 11.1 Elements influencing your brand style

When you operate in the middle of the diagram, where those three elements interlock, you will be developing and adopting a personal visual style, which will have a positive impact on your personal brand.

If you focus on any two but neglect the third, then you are, in my view, missing an opportunity. It's clearly not the end of the world, but this book is about giving you all the advantages you can muster to develop a personal brand in order to achieve what you want. To miss out on exploiting the power of dress and visual presentation is to miss out on the maximum benefit of the whole process.

PERSONAL IDENTITY

Let's look at a few examples, starting with someone who is perhaps an extreme: Lady Gaga. To her fans, she seems edgy, exciting and new. I wouldn't deny her edginess or her ability to generate excitement for a moment, or her talent as a pop writer and performer. What she definitely is not though, is new. Instead, she is working within a well-established tradition of both male and female artists, including, most obviously, David Bowie and Madonna, but embracing many other influences, too.

Gaga's mantra is the expression of personal identity. She tells her fans, 'let your identity be your religion', but she is being a tiny bit disingenuous. Her apparent stance appears to focus fiercely and uncompromisingly on the self-expression element of our three-element model. But she is actually much more considered in her approach. Gaga is thinking very clearly about the responses of her audience (not just her fans but her brand enemies, too). She is thinking hard, too, about her overall strategic intent.

Gaga's appearance and presentation are therefore not just about self-expression, but about the comprehensive building of a brand. Don't get me wrong: I'm not criticizing her for this, but admiring her. David Bowie did precisely the same, as did Madonna and many others.

Let's take another and rather different high-profile example: Apple co-founder and former-CEO Steve Jobs. For years Jobs wore a uniform, as identifiable with him in its way as anything that Lady Gaga wears. Of course a big difference is that whereas Gaga's outfits are ever changing, Jobs' remained resolutely constant for years.

The interesting question to ask is: why? What was Jobs doing with this clothing choice? Or perhaps it's just as useful to ask what was he not doing? The answer is that he was not getting in the way of the communication of his brand and his product. He did not put unnecessary questions or thoughts in our heads about him, and allowed us to focus on the new product or development.

Apple is innovative and changing, and Jobs' unchanging outfit dramatically enhanced that effect. It's also important to note that the elements of his outfit added up to the image of a 'relaxed academic'. It was a little bit geeky, but not too much. Definitely not suited-and-booted, but neither did he try too hard to be 'down with the kids'. The outfit became part of both his personal brand and the Apple brand itself. Like Gaga (although the outcome was dramatically different of course), Jobs was operating at the interface of the three elements: his brand strategy, his intended effect on his audience and his 'personal' style.

There's a very well-known video clip of the former British Prime Minister Tony Blair strolling through the grounds of Camp David on one of his early visits to meet President George W. Bush. You can find the video online, and it's pertinent because it shows two highly prominent figures both failing to follow the three-element principle. Blair in particular looks distinctly uncomfortable and ungainly in his attempt at the relaxed clothing look. My interpretation is that he had thought about the first element (his overall strategy) and the second element (the impression on part of his audience, in this case the President of the USA), but completely disregarded the need to dress in a manner that allowed him to look at ease.

Contrast Blair's approach with Barack Obama's. I don't think there has been a photograph or video yet showing Obama looking anything other than completely at ease with his personal appearance (all three elements in sync) and thus able to focus on the task of being president.

Of course, some people will find this whole thing much easier than others. I take substantial amounts of advice from my wife and daughter to try and get it right for me. It doesn't come naturally at all. But it is always worth the effort.

EXERCISE 14: FINDING YOUR PERSONAL IDENTITY

I would like you now to undertake a very simple exercise, which you might find more productive and beneficial (and somewhat less intimidating) if you do it with the collaboration of a person that you really trust and feel completely at ease with. You need the trust and ease for the simple reason that you'll be thinking about your appearance in terms of what clothes you wear, how you wear your hair and so on. For women, this may include makeup and jewellery. For men it includes beards (beards probably deserve a whole chapter to themselves, but there isn't room in this book) and so on. We are also talking shoes, glasses, bags and other accessories. All the bits that constitute how you appear to other people.

It's a simple exercise but you need to follow the structure carefully to get the benefit.

The first thing you need to understand is that this is not about whether you 'look good'. It doesn't matter whether you are stunningly attractive, or not especially so. It doesn't matter what age you are. And it doesn't matter whether you have plenty of disposable cash or not. Lots of very wealthy people manage to dress very badly.

No, this is about finding a visual presentation of yourself that enhances your personal brand.

OK, now you need to imagine a scenario. Let's start with an interview for a job.

Brand ambition

We are going to start, as ever, with strategy. Think about and write down, as clearly and simply as you can, your objectives in this job interview. Presumably the overarching one will be to get the job, but that's a tad too easy. I want you to go a little deeper. What do you want the interviewers to think and feel about you? I don't want to pre-judge the answer to that, but think about it carefully and note down four things that you want them to think and feel about you from the interview.

Taking the audience view

Now I would like you to step out of your shoes and into theirs. If you were one of them and were interviewing someone for the job in question, what kind of things about a candidate would make you feel positive towards them when they walked in the door? And please don't be saying that you aren't affected by appearances.

Everybody is affected by appearances. Be honest. Write down four characteristics in the appearance of a person coming through the door that would help you to feel positive about them.

Now write down four things that would make you less inclined to think positively about them.

Your personal style and comfort

Now think about how you would be inclined to dress for this interview.

Now here's the wonderfully simple but rather challenging part of the exercise. I want you to actually dress as though you are going to this imaginary interview. Do it without thinking too much about it, but, when you're ready, ask yourself if the way you are presenting yourself matches up to the analysis that you made above.

You can repeat the exercise for other circumstances (a date for example, or a presentation, or a meeting with the bank manager about funds for your business).

And it is very useful to do this exercise with a trusted friend, to give a more objective perspective. Try not to get too emotionally involved in this exercise: this is not the time to be shy or defensive.

REAL-LIFE REINVENTORS ♥
Chris Guillebeau: traveller, entrepreneur and leading blogger

Chris Guillebeau's personal journey started when he became a volunteer for a medical charity in West Africa. 'It was thrilling, challenging and exhausting – all good qualities to have in an adventure,' he says. He gave keynote speeches to presidents, hung out with warlords and professed to have learned more in his four years there than anything he had learned in college. Back in Seattle in 2006, it was hard to settle down to a less exciting life, so Chris took every opportunity to travel while studying international studies on a graduate programme. So far he has visited more than 150 countries and has written about his travels in his blog *The Art of Non-Conformity*. His ultimate aim is to visit every country in the world and to stay self-employed and avoid a 'real job'. To date he is well on the way to achieving this. He says his blog is for those, like himself, who are dissatisfied with conventional beliefs and want to do something remarkable with their lives.

Chapter 13

MUSTERING YOUR BRAND RESOURCES AND USING THEM EFFECTIVELY

No one can do everything they want to do. There aren't enough hours in the day or years in a life. For most people there isn't enough money in the bank either.

We are fundamentally limited by the human condition. We grow up, we grow old, we die. Our years of greatest physical energy are also those of our immaturity and our naivety. Our years of wisdom and experience coincide, frustratingly, with our years of lowered energy and physical potential. As the old joke goes, youth is wasted on the young.

Our talent limits us too, whether God-given or otherwise, depending on your point of view. We can't, in other words, simply decide to be a concert pianist, or an elite athlete, or a millionaire.

Annoying, huh?

I'm not laying out all these truisms because I am a pessimist or a defeatist. Nothing could be further from the truth. I am a card-carrying optimist. In fact, I don't think you can achieve much without optimism in one form or another. So the reason I am stating these grim truths about the human condition is that all of us, in the endeavour of creating a powerful personal brand, need to know precisely where we stand from the beginning. This chapter then is a kind of personal audit of where you are now in all the different aspects that will contribute to the building of your brand.

By the end of this chapter I want you to know exactly what resources you have at your disposal. Picture the creation of your personal brand as setting off on an adventurous journey to an unexplored continent. This chapter is about examining the resources you are likely to need, and comparing them with those you already have at your disposal. I call it a 'brand audit'.

IDENTIFYING YOUR RESOURCES

Resources come in a variety of guises. Very few are material: most are of a different nature. You might call them attitudinal. Money (or the lack of it) is not an obstacle, although many people pretend that it is.

In fact, there are a whole range of things that we are, by nature perhaps, inclined to use as obstacles to our development. We don't have the money. We don't have the time. We don't have the energy. We don't have the talent, the ability, the qualifications, the experience, the credentials, credibility. In short, in my view, we tell ourselves that we don't have permission.

But think for a moment about the people we regard as successes. Whether they are in business, or entertainment, culture, sports or any other field, including spiritual, the people we admire and regard as having 'achieved' have not done so simply because of their giftedness, whether it is physical, artistic or intellectual. And they haven't succeeded because they are just plain wealthy.

Sure, there are people who are born rich, or who get rich, just as there are those who are born with the ability to run very fast or to sing wonderfully or to whack a tennis ball with huge power and an innate hand-eye coordination.

But actually the 'achievers' are not the people who happen to have one or more of these starting-block advantages, but those who take these resources and muster them appropriately.

You don't get to be a tennis star by innate talent alone. You have to take the talent and train it, with extraordinary commitment and sacrifice. You don't build a business empire just by starting off as a rich kid. In fact the media archive is as full of stories of squandered wealth as it is of business success out of nothing.

So, instead of thinking about what you are lacking in terms of talent, wealth, potential, good looks, opportunities and so on, I want you to focus on the resources you actually have, right now. I think you'll find they are much more numerous, powerful and rich with potential than you generally believe.

EXERCISE 15: BRAND RESOURCES AUDIT

The audit model is really a form of questionnaire, but you'll want to note your answers down. It's simple to complete, but as with all the exercises in this book, it will be of most value if you are completely honest with yourself (about your strengths as much as your weaknesses!).

It is worth noting the date of completion, too, because it can be very inspiring and informative to revisit this audit in a few months' or years' time.

I've given a few sample answers to give you the idea, but add as few or as many as are appropriate to your circumstances.

Proven skills and abilities

List specific proven skills and abilities about which you feel real confidence, and indicate your level of ability – from beginner to expert.

> *I can... speak a foreign language to a conversational level.*
>
> *I can... run a spreadsheet programme well enough to manage the accounts of a small business.*
>
> *I can... prepare and present a one-hour workshop for colleagues on my specialist area of work.*

Aptitudes with development potential

List any areas you genuinely feel have some potential but are, as yet, unproven to any great degree.

I could... do great presentations to large audiences if given the opportunity.

I could... manage a team substantially bigger than the one I have at the moment.

I could... be a really good designer if I was able to get some formal training.

Key experiences and achievements

List particular experiences and achievements of which you feel proud and satisfied.

I am proud of... my achievements as a salesperson.

I am proud of... my relationships with my staff team.

I am proud of... my ability to learn new skills very quickly.

Personal qualities and strengths

List personal qualities, strengths and positive attitudes that you feel are deeply true about you, and which you think can be a strong thread going forwards.

I am... very thoughtful and considered, so when I act it is usually very effective.

I am... fearless when it comes to tackling 'difficult' staff situations.

I am... very good at gathering opinions and then drawing sensible conclusions.

Financial resources

Make a note about your financial resources and the freedom this gives you. Stay focused on the positive as far as possible.

> *I have... sufficient income from my part-time job to cover my living costs and commitments, which leaves three days a week free to pursue my dream.*

Discretionary time resources

Make a note about your discretionary time resources. In other words, the times during each week that you have personal control and which you can use to develop yourself and your 'brand'.

> *I can be free on _____ (day) from _____ (time) to _____ (time)*

Health and energy resources

Make a note about your health and energy resources (which will vary according to factors like age, general physical health, disabilities and so on). Again, focus on the positive here.

> *I am... fit, healthy and full of energy.*
> *My... disability restricts my mobility, but I am otherwise in good health.*

Human support resources

Make a note about your support resources and include family, friends, colleagues and mentors from whom you feel you can draw support.

I have... two close friends with whom I can discuss my plans.

My... parents can help me with childcare one day each week.

Other positive resources

Make a note about any other positive resources. These might range from new employment, business or training opportunities, through to an upcoming holiday or trip that you can use as time for reflection and renewal.

Greatest power at your disposal

Make a note of the one thing that you think is your greatest and most powerful 'brand' strength.

I am... really good at solving problems that others find overwhelming.

I am... very calm in a crisis.

I always... make a plan before I begin tasks and somehow that means I always get things done quickly and efficiently.

This audit exercise will give you a couple of sheets of notes that are much more powerful than they may at first appear. Few people take the time or trouble to sit down and consider their situation calmly and rationally, and it has the potential to unlock your new brand for you.

We all know the cliché that one should regret nothing, a view immortalized in song by the great Édith Piaf.

Balanced and healthy people acknowledge that a life will always have regrets. To not regret is to not feel. But the purpose of this book is to limit those regrets in both their number and intensity. Rather more Frank Sinatra (who sang that he had a few regrets, but then again too few to mention) than Piaf.

Completing the brand audit exercise will help you to limit those regrets and to build to a very positive future.

REAL-LIFE REINVENTORS ♀
Mandy Haberman: businesswoman and inventor

Mandy Haberman was a mum with a problem: her daughter was born with a congenital condition called Stickler's Syndrome, which made it difficult to suck from a bottle. Mandy set about inventing a revolutionary new beaker that would be easier to use. Meanwhile, during a visit to the home of another parent and watching their kids spill juice on the carpets, she had another idea. She was inspired to invent the world's first totally leak-proof beaker, which seals between sips. The Anywayup Cup has a controlled valve which only releases its content when sucked. Mandy hadn't planned on going into business with her invention, but the companies she approached to license the product didn't take up the offer, so she started her own company and made it herself. The product has revolutionized the baby/toddler drinking-cup market and solved one of the major headaches of parenthood. Mandy now works tirelessly to help others bring their inventions to the marketplace, and travels the world as a speaker. She has won many design awards and been named British female inventor of the year.

Chapter 14

HOPE, FEAR AND THE CASE FOR RATIONAL OPTIMISM

I hope I have made it clear that I am not a believer in the idea that the universe operates according to the law of attraction. This is the idea behind *The Secret*, and other bestselling books. Their basic tenet is that we attract events and effects which relate directly to the thoughts and feelings we generate. One classic example says that if we worry about the bills then we attract more bills, whereas if we focus our thoughts on wealth, then we become wealthy. If we think about our poor health we become more poorly still, whereas if we focus on health, we attract healthiness.

I have to explain my attitude to this theory with great care: it isn't black and white, and it has some real importance when it comes to thinking about the creation of a personal brand.

So, whether you are an avowed devotee of the law of attraction or think it's a lot of New Age nonsense, please bear with me because I think you'll find it useful ultimately.

For a start, I should be upfront and say that I don't subscribe to the theory of the law of attraction. I don't believe there is any such law in operation. There is nothing in any science, as I understand it, that supports the idea.

Second, I am enormously uncomfortable with the idea that the universe is some kind of reward and punishment machine.

In short, I don't buy it.

And yet...

There is an essential truth at the heart of the attraction theory that is inescapable and highly pertinent to us in the building of a personal brand – it is simply that a positive outlook is enormously beneficial in the brand-building enterprise.

In fact, I'll go further and say that without the adoption of what you might call a positive mindset, you are highly unlikely to succeed in building a personal brand (or any other kind of brand come to that). You don't have to be by nature an optimist. I've met some rather gloomy people who have been very successful in creating personal and business brands. And you don't have to be a 'don't worry, be happy' kind of person either. I've also met successful brand builders who are card-carrying serious worriers that lie awake at night fretting and feeling nauseous.

Success doesn't depend upon your being one of nature's sunny folk. But it does depend upon your willingness and determination (if you happen to be of a melancholy or nervous disposition) to rise above your inclination towards the negative and to act as if you believe absolutely that you will succeed.

I don't mean that you have to pretend to feel confident when you don't. Or that you have to pretend that you believe you will succeed. Or indeed that you have to speak to people as though you are supremely self-assured when in fact you are feeling like jelly inside.

This is not about pretending to feel something inauthentic. It is about behaving as you would behave (doing what you would do) if you actually felt positive, confident and self-assured.

See the difference? I don't care if you carry on feeling vulnerable and weak on the inside, as long as you are being positive on the outside. Well, I do care really, I don't want you to feel bad of course, but you take my point.

This is another place where I differ from the law of attraction aficionados. Their view is that it's what you 'think and feel' that counts, because your thoughts and feelings give off 'energy', which influences outcomes. I believe that it's what you 'do' that makes the difference.

SO, DOES OPTIMISM MATTER?

Yes, it does, because, regardless of whether we feel optimistic or positive, we are aiming at a positive outcome from our actions, and that act of aiming toward the positive is itself a declaration of optimism. By acting as if you expect a positive outcome, you are in a sense (a useful, grounded and rational sense in my view) undertaking a kind of act of faith.

Friends, acquaintances and readers of my books frequently ask me for advice about how they could or should go about starting a business, or reinventing their careers and making other life changes.

This was my key motivator in writing this book: to answer the questions that trouble all those people and which, of course, have endlessly troubled me.

There are many different questions. Some people want to know whether their business idea will succeed. I try to reply honestly that I can't possibly know the answer. I may think the idea is an absolute winner, or the worst business idea I've ever heard. The truth is that I am just as likely to be wrong as I am to be right in either case. Some people push me for an answer. That's difficult. The truth is that no one – and I mean no one – can possibly know which business ideas will fly and which will fall until after the fact.

A more helpful answer, which I increasingly give, though it always requires some explanation, is that it may not be this particular idea that succeeds definitively. It may not be this business that achieves what you are trying to achieve. It may not be this particular job that fulfils you. It may not be this particular relationship that is really the one. This time may not be the time, but that is not the point, because the energy, the desire and the urge towards a positive outcome is such a powerful one that it is of value in and of itself. The energy that drives a move towards the positive is a move against entropy and death, and is thus a very profound thing.

So my answer to you, if you are asking whether your business will succeed or your new job will fulfil you, or how you will know if you have found the right partner this time, is: 'I don't know'. But that's not the right question. The right question is, does the energy driving me in this particular undertaking feel like it is positive, and moving me towards life and away from entropy?

OVERCOMING FEAR

Other questions I'm asked by people concern the anxieties and fears of undertaking the action of which they dream. All of us dream of desires and ambitions, but it is so easy to let our dreams be overwhelmed by our fears.

We dream of starting a small business, but fear that we will lose our home and savings, and the security of a job that we have grown to hate, and this often contributes to our self-loathing.

We dream of finding a life partner with whom we can form a lasting relationship built on the solid foundations of love, friendship and respect. Yet we fear desperately that others will find us inadequate, unattractive or dull, and that ultimately we will be betrayed or otherwise disappointed.

In short, it is all too easy to be transfixed, pinned to the spot, desperate to make positive change but so anxious of the perceived risks involved. We fear the future. We fear the past. We fear the present. We fear ourselves.

Anxiety and its big ugly brother fear are unavoidable. We can't kill them. We can't, by an act of will, make them cease to exist. We can, however, on occasion, outsmart them.

Anyone who embarks upon any kind of enterprise (artistic, commercial, romantic, whatever) is setting off on a journey in time, down a particular and unknown path. We all know, whether we understand much about physics or not, that time's arrow can only travel in one direction. And so our journey, in a profound and existential sense, is an important one. The time and energy we commit to it can never be regained. We can stop and change direction, or even try to go back to where we began, though of course we can never truly go back. We will be older, possibly wiser, with more or less energy, with more or less money, with more experience: but we will be changed. And the world will have changed, too. So every undertaking we embark upon is undeniably significant.

And when we set off (or in some cases prevaricate about setting off to the point of stasis, never actually leaving), we always have two companions with us.

The first companion, and the one we try to keep closest to us as our guide and inspiration, is Hope. Hope that we will succeed in our business. Hope that we may get that job. Hope that we can become affluent. Hope that we will be loved. Hope helps us pack our bag for the adventure. Hope is always bouncing around with enthusiasm and passion. Hope thinks everything is going to turn out just fine. Hope knows you're unstoppable.

But our second companion is always there too, picking over and criticizing every item that Hope puts in our bag. Criticizing. Grumbling. Predicting failure. This second companion is Fear. You'd much prefer that Fear would get lost. You don't want Fear on your adventure. He's not liked by anybody and he's not welcome. But there's no avoiding it: Fear is coming with you, because Fear, just like Hope, is part of you.

This is the inevitable truth. The bottom line is that if you ever try to do anything of significance in your life, from asking someone out on a date to launching a new business, you will feel both hope and fear. You may call them something different. Some actors and performers feel physically sick before they step onto the stage, though they may be hugely talented, popular and experienced. Some people stay in a job they hate for 30 years rather than feel the anxiety of changing. Some people go to their grave never having been able to ask another person to go out for dinner with them. All because Fear got the upper hand. Fear told them the adventure was too dangerous. Too risky. Not worth it. Was bound to end in disappointment.

For others (fewer in number, I suspect), Hope becomes the dominant player and Fear is banished. And some of these people, heady with the triumph of defeating Fear, like Icarus, fly too close to the sun. They invest everything they own in an ill-conceived business concept. They risk their home, their savings, their marriage because they truly believe in their 'destiny'. Others queue up to audition for a TV talent show, convinced that because their desire is strong, and because they have conquered Fear with Hope, they will succeed.

On a less ambitious scale, thousands and thousands of people go to job interviews without preparing, because they believe it is possible, or even preferable, to 'wing it', to rely on their personality shining through.

MANAGING FEAR AND HOPE

My point is, counter-intuitive though it may seem, that conquering Fear by Hope can be as counter-productive and problematic as allowing Fear to destroy Hope.

We need Fear. Fear is the companion who grabs us and pulls us back from the edge when we are about to step over because we are blindly running along with Hope, not looking where we are going.

But Fear is also a tyrant. Fear is so risk-averse that he will never let us do anything other than follow the well-worn paths we have trod before. Even then, Fear is only at peace when we avoid the ones that have proved risky or dangerous in the past.

So what should we do about Hope and Fear in our endeavours to create a personal brand, to make positive change in our lives? What is the sensible person to do about these powerful forces that accompany us everywhere?

My belief is that we have to live with them but manage them. They are both a part of us, but they must not individually be allowed the power to define us or to drive us.

I used to say to people who were thinking of starting a business that they would have to learn to live with a constant state of low-level anxiety. But that was an inadequate description in various ways. Partly because the anxiety isn't always low level – it's sometimes acute and terrifying. Many entrepreneurs and others will recognize the trauma of waking suddenly at three in the morning in a panic attack, breathless, nauseous, heart racing, shaking with the fear of impending disaster (financial or otherwise). Thankfully, those acute episodes, when Fear manages to grab the reins and to gallop through your subconscious, are rare for most of us. But many of us will experience them from time to time.

But it was also an inadequate description because it doesn't account for the times when euphoric Hope takes over: when you feel that you are on a roll, can do no wrong, are indestructible. You have only to read the newspapers or watch the TV news to see almost daily accounts of high-profile individuals, and often their businesses, who have fallen victim to this triumph of Hope, leading them, siren-like, onto the rocks of bad investment decisions, personal infidelities, hubristic takeovers, poorly thought-through product launches, ego-driven solo projects, or crushingly money-wasting research and development programmes.

Hope, given its head, is as dangerous as Fear unbound.

This is the reason why this chapter is called rational optimism.

The personal brand builder, like you and me, needs both Hope and Fear. And we need to keep them in balance. Hope drives us when Fear would keep us trapped, like the rabbit in oncoming headlights. But Fear also puts out an arm and stops us from stepping out into traffic.

So, the personal brand builder has to believe, deep inside, that they can triumph: by applying their character, their story, their unique brand promise, they can achieve the goals for which they strive. But by acknowledging the existence and role of Fear, they will make better, wiser decisions, and they will make progress in a way that is unachievable by so many people queuing up for talent shows or asking the universe for abundance.

EXERCISE 16 : BALANCING HOPE AND FEAR

This is a simple but rather profound exercise to close this chapter.

I would like you, as simply and as clearly as you can, to list your Hopes and Fears. They can be of any nature: fears about dating, fears about your business, fears about money, or health, or anything else. List your Hopes, too. Your hopes about your career, hopes about making meaning from your life.

Simply describe them in a few words. You don't need to analyse or explain them. This is just for you.

Now, if you'd like, I want to suggest something slightly more challenging. It doesn't matter if it seems too tough. Come back to it later, perhaps. But if you persist, I think you'll find it revealing and helpful.

Take one of your Hopes and describe it as honestly as you can. Then, by way of contrast, describe the Fear that provides its counterpoint. Finally, describe the reality of the 'balance' between the Hope and the Fear.

FINDING BALANCE

It is all too easy for either your Hope or your Fear to run amok! They are both dangerous if unchecked, which is why I think the idea of balance is such a powerful and helpful one.

Balance is where you can find stability and strength to pursue any kind of venture, enterprise or endeavour.

To help, I will give you an example of my own (which I am curiously anxious about sharing, but heck we're all in this together).

One of my hopes over several years has been that my roots band The Proposition could become a credible act and play alongside some top-class artists at festivals and get established on the folk/country/ roots circuit of clubs and other venues.

One of my fears is that these musical ambitions are based on fairly limited musical ability, which limits our chances of success in a fiercely competitive youth-oriented musical world.

The balancing thought, which my band compadres and I keep in our heads, is that we have evidence that people actually like our music. We have had good reviews in numerous magazines and we get regular bookings at small festivals and clubs. For all our self-doubts, we are able to remind ourselves there is proven merit and real personal reward in our endeavours. You don't have to be famous, or even professional, for playing in a band to be a life-enhancing buzz!

REAL-LIFE REINVENTORS ♈
Scott Harrison: founder of charity: water

Scott Harrison was a New York nightclub promoter and self-confessed hedonist. Then, at the age of 28, partying hard on a beach in Uruguay with the 'right people' and copious amounts of drugs, he had an epiphany: he was selfish and needed to change his life. Back home, he volunteered on a hospital ship in West Africa for two years, photographing the work of doctors as they treated patients with facial tumours. Inspired by the difference he had seen this charity making to people's lives, Scott set up his own campaigning and fundraising organization called charity: water. Its aim is to help the billion people around the world who still don't have access to safe, clean drinking water. He has targeted the same wealthy set he originally socialized with: those willing to spend their dollars on expensive drinks in nightclubs. He launched the charity with a cool party and raised funds from selling tickets. His funky, stylish charity pledges to give 100 per cent of donations to fund clean drinking water projects and has raised millions for the cause.

Chapter 15

YOUR 'CUSTOMER EXPERIENCE': HOW TO MAKE IT A GOOD ONE

Popular wisdom has it that Britain is very poor at customer service and that, in the USA, they have this skill nailed. But I think it's too easy, and erroneous, to make such sweeping generalizations.

The best hospitality service I ever received until recently was on Emirates and Etihad airlines, who seem to want to try to outdo each other in helpfulness and passenger care, and at Rotana hotels in Abu Dhabi and Dubai.

But even their impressive efforts were outdone (for me at least) by the warmth, charm and consistently high standards shown by staff at the Kempinski Hotel in Berlin. The hotel staff were unfailingly polite, helpful, cheery and sincere, without being fawning, which is pretty much all you could hope for from a hotel.

But the most outstanding bit of customer service that I've ever experienced, which was substantially above and beyond the call of duty, came from a Sikh yellow cab driver in New York. For reasons which I won't bore you with, a few years ago, on a visit to Manhattan, I ran out of cash at the same time as having my cards fail on me. Needing a cab to JFK airport from Midtown Manhattan, a journey which at that time cost around $35, I explained to the driver that I had only $25, and requested that he take me as far as that amount would carry me (fully expecting that I would have to walk the last few kilometres).

Nevertheless, without comment, he drove me all the way to the terminal, and when I handed over my less-than-adequate $25 with embarrassed apologies, he promptly gave me $5 back. Before I could challenge him the cabbie explained that it was unfair to expect anyone to spend a couple of hours in an airport without a cup of coffee. I protested that he was being too generous, and he countered that I could repay him 'in another life'.

'Repay me in another life,' is not the kind of comment you hear very often from taxi drivers, or anyone else in the service sector, but wouldn't the world be rather lovely if it happened more often?

This driver wasn't trying to promote his cab firm, and I don't think for a moment he had been trained or briefed to provide cheap rides and cashback to English travellers too incompetent to look after their finances. His extraordinary customer service didn't come from a training programme or customer experience guidelines, but from somewhere else altogether, but what a job this guy did, and on so many fronts.

In one act of simple generosity and non-judgemental customer-focus, this guy cemented my love for NYC itself. He did a great 'brand' job, too, for NYC yellow taxi drivers, and a pretty good one for Sikhism. I've told this story to hundreds of people directly, and to thousands via my books.

But hang on, you might well be thinking, how did this guy's generosity help him develop his 'brand'? Did he get a better job as a result? Did he benefit directly in any way? Well, the short answer to that is that I am absolutely willing to bet that his enjoyment of his job, even his sense of personal fulfilment if you like, is of a higher degree than that of another driver who might have taken a quite different attitude to the exact same situation.

I am also willing to bet that this guy's positive and pragmatic outlook ensures he enjoys more positive relationships, not only with customers, but also with his employer and work colleagues. Providing a positive 'customer experience', in other words, is an all-round beneficial undertaking for all concerned.

EVERYONE'S A CUSTOMER

My perception of customer service in general is that it has become polarized in recent years. With many large businesses and organizations there has been substantial effort, spend and training on all aspects of the customer experience, with noticeable results. So service in the larger retail chains and other service organizations seems to have clearly improved in the UK.

But this is frequently not the case with many other chains and, indeed, with many small independent businesses, in all kinds of sectors. There are exceptions of course: small firms that are passionately committed to giving the customer a fantastic experience. But it is all too easy for this element to be overlooked, and for the customer to be at the very end of the list of priorities, if present at all.

A few years ago I worked closely with a 'customer experience' team at a large UK insurance company. The team had grown out of what had previously been the 'complaints department', whose *raison d'être* had of course been to placate upset and angry customers. Starting on the wrong foot you might say. But the new version of this team had a mission, which was 'to bring the company closer to the customer'. It was a powerful, energized and highly influential team, with a strong and inspiring leader. Considering the size of the company this little team had a major task on its hands, but from what I saw it made a real and positive impact on customers (and thus on the success of the brand) by helping the company to focus on that elusive notion of customer experience.

Customer experience really matters in business today. Great brands can't grow and thrive without it. But why should it matter to you?

It matters to you - whether you are an employee, an entrepreneur, or looking for a job or a promotion, or a partner - for the very simple reason that, in the end, the only thing you can actually give to another person (in any of these contexts: business, social or even romantic) is an 'experience'.

Strange as it may seem when thinking of yourself as an individual, everyone you encounter can be thought of as being your 'customer'. You may not be selling them something, or giving them any kind of service, but just by engaging with them, on any level, you are certainly providing an experience.

You have a simple choice. You can endeavour to make that experience a positive one, even a brilliant and life-enhancing one, or you can choose not to bother. But if the whole premise of individual as brand is a useful one for people like me and you, which I absolutely believe that it is, then it follows that, like commercial or organizational brands, we too have a responsibility to give our 'customers' a positive experience.

The benefits of doing so are huge, and I don't need to list them, but it's worth emphasizing that these benefits are both internal and external.

I mean by 'internal', as illustrated by the NYC taxi driver story, that there is something deeply pleasurable, satisfying and intrinsically positive for you in the act of giving someone else a positive experience. Is it not a pleasure to be thanked by a stranger on the street when you have given them directions? Is it not a pleasure to see the delight on the face of someone for whom you have arranged a surprise, no matter how modest? Of course it is. There is nothing controversial or challengeable in the notion that the creation of happiness in others provides happiness to the creator. It is, in my view, self-evident, but (happily) it seems also to be supported by scientific studies (of which there are an increasing number) focusing on the psychology of happiness.

So, let's take it as read that we as individuals will do our inner selves a power of good by providing a good customer experience to others. But let's also remember, to come back to a theme that I have touched on elsewhere in this book, that providing this positive experience doesn't happen automatically or by accident and that therefore it isn't enough just to always 'be one's self'. I don't want you to be someone else, or to be phoney, or to try so hard that you come across as a manipulator. Be authentic, but also be attentive to the needs of the moment.

Imagine yourself in a shop. Any shop. You want some advice on a product before you purchase it. Is it your hope that the sales assistant is true to themselves and their mood at the time, or that (regardless of how they actually feel) they make the effort to focus on you and your needs? It's the latter of course.

Close friendship and partner relationships are different of course. We can let our emotions hang out with some people close to us, some of the time. But even then one has to be attentive to the moment and the needs of the moment. Nobody fancies a moody git for long, do they?

And, outside of those close relationships, attentiveness becomes even more important: because the impact of the customer experience you create can and will have a direct effect upon how you are perceived, how well you are liked, how much you are valued and, in the end, how long you are going to hold onto your job, or your business.

I am not suggesting that we all go round with pleasant glassy smiles on our faces, pretending to be happy bunnies all of the time. Of course not. What I am saying, however, is that attentiveness to your impact on the experience of others (and your adjustment of behaviour accordingly), makes a difference, to you and your emotions, and to you and your opportunities and prospects.

If you buy the notion that everyone you encounter is in a sense your customer, which I hope you do, then how should that affect how you interact with him or her.

ATTENTIVENESS

The first key element, as I've mentioned, is 'attentiveness'. All I mean by this is simply to pay heed to each encounter to a degree that is just a little more heightened than your natural, ordinary, day-to-day level.

It has something in common with the Buddhist idea of being in the moment, or mindfulness. We are so inclined to be busy, distracted, self-absorbed or otherwise inattentive, that it is incredibly easy to miss opportunities to provide good 'customer experience'.

I am quite a shy person and find some social situations quite challenging, even intimidating. These vary for me from drinks receptions (I'm really bad at those and I'm the antithesis of a good mingler), through to simple encounters in the street with people who I know but haven't seen for a long time. I become (and I'm embarrassed now, just thinking about it) awkward, self-conscious and shy in these situations, and I know I'm not alone in feeling that way.

This is a personality trait that would be terribly difficult to change and, actually, I have no desire to change my personality. So, instead, I am trying to follow my own advice of attentiveness. Being aware of my shyness in the situation, but also (and this is the important bit) being aware that this affects my behaviour, and thus affects, perhaps negatively, my impact on others, helps me to address both the feeling of shyness and the behaviour.

In other words, by being attentive to the situation, I understand and accept the importance of the way that I operate, and thus I am inclined to operate a little differently, a little more positively, than had I not been paying such attention.

By contrast, we all know people who are so socially self-assured that they will fill any given social encounter with conversation, news, jollity and energy. Sometimes that's enjoyable. But often, the apparent ease of people with this degree of self-confidence is intimidating, tedious or irritating to others. Equally, the socially self-confident among us need to heighten their attentiveness and to adjust their behaviour accordingly – to give a more positive and empathetic customer experience.

It is not just in chance social situations that this attentiveness idea can improve the experience we give to others. It is, arguably, even more significant when we get to encounters online, whether on social media or via email.

The trouble with the online encounter is that, by definition, it is not supported by all the non-verbal elements that are available in a face-to-face or even phone encounter.

This makes it staggeringly easy to offend people unintentionally, to be misunderstood without being aware that you have been misunderstood, to appear aggressive when you simply mean to be direct, and so on.

Millions of people are completely at ease with cyber communications and it may well be that it has a levelling effect, allowing many people to communicate more easily than by the old offline channels. But I believe my point about attentiveness and providing a positive customer experience still stands. I know enough about social media to know it is a 'place' where it is easy to believe the ordinary rules don't apply. A place where you can say and do anything without heed to any consequences.

Attentiveness is required even more in the online environment perhaps, because, unlike a clumsy encounter at a party or on the street, an ugly spat on Twitter doesn't go away easily, or in some senses, at all, and the audience is potentially just a tad larger.

EMPATHY

Attentiveness is really just the first element in providing a positive customer experience. The second crucial element is empathy: the ability and willingness to see the world from another's point of view.

It is empathy, combined with attentiveness, which allows us to understand that our shyness might lead us to avoid eye contact with someone we know on the street, but know that it may not seem like shyness to them, but rather more like a kind of insult, a passive-aggressive act.

It is empathy that should inform the super confident to stop talking for a little while in order to allow others to speak.

It is empathy that in a work situation will prompt you to put aside what you are doing in order to help a colleague who is struggling.

And it is empathy that should allow us to understand that someone who is upset or angry with us may well have sound reason from their point of view, even though we may feel affronted and defensive.

There is no great secret to empathy, except that it demands you temporarily step out of yourself and into the shoes of another. It isn't easy to do, but it isn't complex either. I believe empathy is more an act of will than a particular skill, which is to say that you can choose to be empathetic or you can choose not to bother. It is crucial in the commercial world, and it is part of the power of the most successful brands. But it is also desperately important to you in building your own personal brand. People are drawn inexorably towards those who exhibit and demonstrate empathy, and they tend to shy away from those who don't.

FOCUS

The third element of customer experience is to focus on a positive outcome. It's the word 'focus' that is most important here. If we are not interested in reinventing ourselves, fulfilling our personal potential and achieving, at least in part, the things of which we dream, then focus is not required. For that matter, neither is attentiveness or empathy.

If, on the other hand, you are reading this book because you do actually want to make positive change - to travel in the direction of your dreams, rather than drift like a cork on the waves - then focus becomes critical.

If attentiveness in this context refers to being aware of the importance and the latent potential in the moment, present in every encounter, then focus in this context refers to the future, after the encounter.

And, as the term 'customer experience' implies, the focus is on the other party's outcome not yours. We are building a brand, not doing a deal. We are creating meaning, not ducking and diving. Your focus in every encounter should be on a positive outcome for the 'customer'.

That positive outcome can take any number of forms. It doesn't have to be action-oriented. I am not talking about networking or schmoozing here; I am talking about leaving your 'customer' in a positive state of being. You can simply leave someone with a smile on his or her face, having enjoyed a chat. That's an achievement in the frantic world of today. Or you can leave them feeling that you were genuinely interested in their news, good or bad. You can leave them feeling supported. You can leave them with an idea. You can leave them with a warm glow!

Actually, you may not even know how you have left them. But if you focus your intent on leaving them with a positive outcome, rather than on taking something for yourself, then you will, however subtly, have enhanced your own brand.

Your 'brand' is simply a shorthand term for the set of meanings that you create in the hearts and minds of others. And there is no more powerful way to do that every day than to treat each person as a customer, and therefore:

- To be attentive to the moment of the interaction and its meanings for them;
- To be empathetic to them and their view, and to adjust your behaviour accordingly;
- To be focused on leaving them with a positive outcome from your encounter.

EXERCISE 17: CREATING POSITIVE OUTCOMES

Think about the encounters you have in your life and about how you can use attentiveness, empathy and focus to enhance future encounters and, in doing so, build your brand. You might find the following questions useful in thinking about your aspects of 'customer service' in a particular encounter scenario:

- *How attentive am I in this situation as a rule?*
- *How can I raise my attentiveness in this encounter?*
- *How empathetic am I usually in this encounter?*
- *How can I demonstrate increased empathy in this encounter?*

- *How much am I usually focused on a positive outcome for the other person (or people) in this encounter?*

- *What would be required to give them a positive outcome next time we meet?*

REAL-LIFE REINVENTORS ▼
Kazumi Izaki: housewife and professional female boxer

During the day, Kazumi Izaki's life is like that of any other suburban Tokyo housewife and mother. She wakes at 5:45 a.m. then cleans, shops for ingredients and prepares meals. But in the evening, after cooking dinner for her husband and two daughters, she heads to the gym and is transformed into one of the oldest professional female boxers in the world. Now in her late forties, she follows a punishing two-hour evening training regime and spars with men half her age. She has broken her eye socket and nose several times, but the injuries just make her tougher. Competing as a flyweight boxer, she is almost double the age of many of her opponents. It all started more than a decade ago when Kazumi, an ex-aerobics instructor, took up boxercise to get fit. She soon became addicted and took up the real sport with a debut fight in 2001. She is reputed to have a powerful left hook, despite her apparently light frame, and claims her body is in the best shape ever after years of workouts.

Chapter 16

WHAT TO DO WHEN YOUR BRAND GETS IT WRONG (WHICH IT WILL)

There are few more disturbing experiences than the realization that you have let someone down, inadvertently caused hurt or upset, or simply made some kind of blunder that cannot fail but be noticed. With such failures, which are frequently not of our own making (or rather not of our intended making), comes the desperate burden of embarrassment and its big ugly brother, shame.

In our efforts to build our personal brand reputation it is easy to focus on the positive and on achieving positive impacts on others. Of course that is what we want and need to achieve. But in this chapter, and strangely I feel the need to apologize for this (there's human nature for you), we are going to address the inevitability of occasional failure.

Whether you are running a business, doing your damnedest to be the rising star of your organization, or just trying to be the most engaging and attractive you can be to others, you will, at some point, fall over (quite possibly literally, and definitely figuratively).

The question is: what should you do when that happens? Well, actually the question is better stated as what should you do 'before' it happens, as well as 'when'. Happily the answer is simple, but it's one that so many people and organizations find difficult to put into action.

The answer is four-fold: and it is four crucial parts of a process. If you follow the process properly you can turn a bad situation into a better one, but you can also go considerably further and enhance your brand reputation, taking it to a higher level than it was before the problem arose.

So please try to view the process as a hugely positive experience. It may not always feel that way at the time, and for many it will feel emotionally challenging, but I can guarantee, nay promise you, that it is effective and infinitely more beneficial than the traditional methodology of burying your head in the sand, or defiantly refusing to admit that you've got it wrong.

First and foremost, you have to acknowledge there is a problem. And you have to acknowledge it clearly, swiftly and in terms that allow the other person to understand and believe you are being genuine in your acknowledgement.

The second stage of the process is the apology itself. Saying sorry is desperately painful and difficult for some people, and yet others seem to be almost addicted to apologizing. What is actually needed is moderation. The apology-refuser needs to realize the extraordinary power of saying sorry, and the apology-addict needs to understand that saying sorry when it's not necessary or appropriate undermines the effect of the apology when it *is* required.

The third stage of the process is the 'putting right' of the problem. Critical, but so often neglected.

And the final stage is the re-establishment of your relationship with the person or people involved. This last stage is the one that most brands, and most individuals, forget.

WHEN MAJOR BRANDS GET IT WRONG

One of the most famous brand mess-ups was Coca-Cola's extraordinary decision to replace its globally loved 'secret' recipe for its market-leading drink with an 'improved' recipe. After years of market dominance, the Coca-Cola bosses felt suddenly and dramatically threatened by a brilliant marketing initiative carried out by its arch rival Pepsi.

What Pepsi had discovered, and then went on to exploit in a global advertising campaign, was that in blind taste testings the taste of Pepsi was significantly rated preferable to that of Coke.

Pepsi turned this research finding into what they called 'The Pepsi Challenge', repeating the blind taste tests on camera over and over again.

As a direct result, Pepsi's market share increased substantially, and it appeared that at last there existed a major potential threat to Coke's dominance. Coca-Cola's executives panicked and, after a major market research project, they concluded that cola drinkers seemed to prefer a drink that was a little sweeter (and more like Pepsi) than the long-standing Coke product. Reading the research at face value led them famously to kill off the much-loved Coke product and to replace it with New Coke.

Much to Coca-Cola's shock and horror, the initiative proved dramatically unpopular. Within days of the announcement there were huge protests outside the company's headquarters. Bottles of New Coke were emptied into drains in front of TV cameras, and petitions were signed *en masse* to demand the reintroduction of the original Coke.

This is a well-known story in the world of branding and marketing, but it is usually viewed and described as a brand disaster for Coke. The reality, however, is not quite that simple, and that's because of Coca-Cola's response. The initial reaction of the company's senior executives was a kind of dumbfounded resistance to the reality, as though they simply could not believe what was happening.

But to their credit, and this is why the story has relevance for us here, the brand managers realized that what they had to do was admit they had made a mistake and apologize. What they had neglected to think through in launching New Coke was that the millions of Coke drinkers worldwide were not just buying a sweet fizzy brown liquid (if that was the case then improving its taste would have been positive and unproblematic), but were actually buying into a complicated and emotionally charged brand concept.

To put it another way, Coca-Cola had under-estimated the value of its own brand. Once the strength of feeling was recognized, realization dawned and the company made the brave decision to admit it had been wrong, to apologize to its loyal consumers and reintroduce the original formula.

It followed, in other words, the first steps of the process I have outlined. Acknowledge the problem. Say you're sorry. Put the problem right.

The fourth step for Coke, that of re-establishing its relationships with its customers over the longer term, fell almost effortlessly out of the company's swift apology and course correction. Coke was a much-loved brand: the most recognized brand in the world. One might say (to borrow from Kevin Roberts again) that it had a great deal of love in the bank.

The result, therefore, far from being a brand disaster in the long term, demonstrated that Coca-Cola listened to, respected and responded to its customers, and this seemed to make those customers feel even more positive towards the brand.

Coke remains the world's greatest brand on virtually every measure. It has gone on to successfully introduce numerous new flavours. But it has never again considered withdrawing its beloved core product.

It's a story with a happy ending but it's not difficult to imagine a very different outcome if the company's bosses had decided to dig in their heels and ignore the protests. In that case I am not sure that Coca-Cola would exist as we know it today.

PERSONALITIES MESS UP, TOO

By contrast, there are numerous examples of brands and brand-personalities not quite getting the apology right. In early 2010 the great golfer Tiger Woods was forced to face up to the scandal of his private life. A few weeks into the story Woods made an apology at a press conference, but it was an unsatisfactory affair (excuse the pun) because it somehow didn't seem completely sincere. It may well have been utterly genuine, but the manner in which the press conference was controlled and delivered did not swiftly heal Woods' reputation. When it was followed, shortly afterwards, by a TV commercial for Nike featuring a silent Woods staring into the camera with a voiceover from the golfer's dead father, the level of puzzlement increased.

Tiger Woods' brand was not destroyed by the scandal, but it was clearly compromised. It would have been easier and more effective for him to adopt a clearer and less enigmatic approach to apologizing for the genuine disappointment felt by his many fans and admirers.

Sometimes an apology won't fix the situation – not because of a lack of sincerity, but because it is the apology and not the original offence which seems to be the exception rather than the norm. Former British Prime Minister Gordon Brown insulted a voter after a meeting during the 2010 election campaign, thinking that he was speaking privately to an aide. His words were caught on tape and the story went global. Brown was clearly mortified by what he had done and was deeply remorseful. He met with the insulted voter and apologized, both privately and publicly. It was a heartfelt and convincing acknowledgement of a major error. But a general election campaign has a pace of change to it, and of course a relentlessly constant media coverage which makes recovery much more difficult than in 'normal' circumstances.

Few observers doubted Brown's sincerity in apologizing, but, more importantly, the incident seemed to cement his reputation for emotional outbursts and what can only really be described as 'grumpiness'. In Brown's case the incident was not seen therefore as a one-off, out-of-character moment, but rather as a window into his personality.

Many people believe the incident played a substantial part in his losing of the election. So what could Brown possibly have done to save the situation? Well, strange though this may sound, the work really needed to have been done in advance. Had the Prime Minister's general demeanour been perceived as warmer, more relaxed, less judgemental and more open, the incident may well have been forgiven, or could at least have had a rather less negative impact.

I am not suggesting that Gordon Brown should have changed his personality, but perhaps he should have put compensating elements in place.

Two final brief examples of how not to put things right when you get things wrong. Sir Fred Goodwin, former chief executive of the UK bank RBS, when faced with the media furore over his extraordinary bonus payments at a time when the bank was collapsing and being bailed out by the government, was not only unapologetic, but actually defiant and combative.

You could argue that the reputation of RBS couldn't be adversely affected any more than it already was, but Goodwin's attitude did damage on a wider scale, and cemented the image of the greedy banker from which the whole finance industry will take a long time to recover.

And another British company, sadly, had its moment of gross mishandling of a bad situation when BP's exploratory platform exploded in the Gulf of Mexico, creating a vast oil spillage that did huge damage all along the Gulf coast. Chief Executive Tony Hayward showed a remarkable lack of sensitivity to the tragic deaths of several rig workers, as well as the ongoing environmental disaster (and its effects on the livelihoods of thousands of people), when he was famously quoted as saying, 'I just want my life back'. He and the corporation made numerous apologies at the time, but they all seemed insincere and unconvincing compared to this personal statement.

A year or so after the incident, when thankfully the oil leak had been stemmed and the massive clear up considered to be largely successful, BP once again threatened to damage its own fragile brand by running an expensive advertising campaign praising its efforts and achievements in the clean up. It had achieved much, of course, but many felt it was a little early for the company to be switching from apology mode to blowing its own trumpet.

So how long do you need to go on apologizing? The simple answer, honestly, is 'long enough'. It is impossible to be more precise than that. But at some point, if you are sensitive to your audience, you will know when you have been forgiven. This happens in personal, as well as business, relationships, too.

Let's leave the famous brands and personalities for a while and get back to thinking about what we actually need to do when things go wrong and look at the four-stage process in more detail.

Stage one: Acknowledging

We become aware of our shortcomings in a variety of ways. Sometimes we have one of those 'Oh no!' moments when we realize before anyone else does that we have made some kind of ghastly error. We make an offhand comment, which we know, almost even before it leaves our lips, will cause hurt or offence. We send a grumbling email to a colleague in which we are rude about an annoying client but we inadvertently copy in the client. I should add that I haven't actually done this myself (honestly), but I have seen it done. In fact, I have seen it done twice by senior people in companies where I have worked. In one case it led to instant resignation, and in the other to a very narrow escape (when the sender managed to persuade the client's PA to delete the email from their boss's inbox, without reading it).

Now an offensive email is going to get found very swiftly in most cases, so you might wonder what the role of the 'acknowledgement' stage is in this case. But that would be to miss the point of the acknowledgement. Acknowledgement is the stage at which you make the other person aware that you are aware there is a problem. It's important because it not only marks your understanding of their feelings, wants and needs, and their right to be treated well, but also demonstrates your willingness to lower your defences and your guard.

Acknowledgement is, in effect, the preliminary to apologizing. It is an important preliminary though, because without it the apology will appear either automatic and glib, or considered and artificial.

To give you an example: a little while ago my daughter was in a nightclub and banged her head on the corner of a fuse box. She is not particularly tall, and this was at the beginning of the evening not the end, if you get my drift. It wasn't her fault and it turned out that another customer had done the same thing moments earlier.

She was in pain, as well as slightly shocked, but when she complained that the box should be marked or moved she was treated brusquely and told to look where she was going. Needless to say, no apology was forthcoming, but what she wanted was an acknowledgement that there was a problem.

It was a simple thing to want really, but she didn't get it. Instead, she has doubtless told many people about the incident, which can't help but cast the club in a negative light.

Acknowledgement is not the same as apology, but it is crucial. Don't neglect to do it when it's called for.

Stage two: Apologizing

This is the most vital and the most emotionally challenging of the four stages. There is only one way to apologize, and that is unreservedly. If you are ever tempted to put your apology in any other terms than that, then please pause, and resist that urge.

If you, as a business or an individual, say wholeheartedly and sincerely that you personally (note 'you', not 'we' or 'on behalf of') are sorry for what you (note 'you') have done, then you stand a very good chance of being forgiven (criminal acts aside of course). But if your apology is mealy mouthed and half-hearted, which says you are sorry for any hurt that the other party felt (in other words transferring the weight of the whole thing from your shoulders onto theirs), you won't be forgiven but resented and quite possibly scorned. Sadly, many apologizers tend to take this stance. They say they are sorry that we are unhappy, but they don't say sorry for what they have actually done, or failed to do; an apology without an acknowledgement in other words. It won't cut the mustard and it will further damage your brand rather than enhance it.

By contrast, a real apology, genuinely felt and given, will in most cases be genuinely felt and received.

Stage three: Mending

An apology for one offence (of whatever kind) won't be of very much value unless you make sure that the wrong is righted swiftly and definitively. If you have to apologize for the simple offence of being late for a meeting (or a date) there is probably not much harm done, provided you acknowledge and apologize as we have already discussed. But if you follow that apology by being similarly late on the next occasion, your initial apology will look hollow and pointless.

In other words, if and when you let someone down and it is appropriate to acknowledge that and apologize for it, it is also appropriate to put something in place to make sure you don't have to apologize again for the same thing. If you have a tendency to be late (as I do, I'm sorry to say) then set your watch earlier or set an alarm which prompts you to leave earlier, or just learn to tell yourself to stop whatever you are doing in time to allow you to get wherever it is you are supposed to be. I say this with real conviction because lateness is a deep-rooted character trait in me. Not because I'm lazy, but because I try to do too much.

And I, like you, would find it difficult or impossible to change my character. I can't really. And neither can you. But we can change our behaviour. So I am still a late-arriver by nature, but I have taught myself (almost) to arrive on time, despite that character trait.

Stage four: Rebuilding

This is the neglected stage of the process, and I think it is neglected more because of anxiety than anything else, particularly in personal relationships. It's a little too easy, after you have acknowledged, apologized and mended the offence, to think that the job is done.

But the critical mistake we make in this assumption is that just because the issue or incident is no longer being spoken of, that it is no longer being felt. Still waters run deep and although the apology may have taken a lot of effort, it may nevertheless not have been conclusive to the other person.

You can't, in my view, just move on, and you can't expect the other person to do so either. There is a truth in marketing and customer research (which it took many companies a long time to come to terms with) that a lack of customer complaints does not mean your customers are happy. In fact, it's worse news than that. Customer satisfaction surveys frequently indicate that customers are a lot of happy bunnies, while the reality is that they are leaving in their droves.

The human truth behind this is that people are not generally inclined to tell you about their true feelings, especially when those feelings are negative. Particularly when you have hurt them or let them down.

The answer to this problem is to understand and act on the need for a sustained period of rebuilding. To put it simply, you have to go on a kind of journey with the person or people concerned, demonstrating over a period of time (the exact length of which will depend on your relationship and the circumstances) that you are committed to them and by acting appropriately with them.

It is only by fulfilling this part of the process that you will actually rebuild the relationship solidly, and with it your 'brand' in their eyes.

If you make that commitment, you will achieve that aim, and you will know when you have done so.

REAL-LIFE REINVENTORS ♥
William Kamkwamba: eco-hero

As a young boy in Malawi, William Kamkwamba was forced to quit school in 2001 when the family's maize crop failed and they could no longer afford the fees. But William refused to give up his education: he visited the library in his spare time and read books on science. One in particular captured his imagination. It showed how windmills could be used to generate electricity and pump water and so he set about building one for himself. At the age of 14, he figured out how to construct the frame and mechanics, and scoured a local scrapyard for components, including an old bicycle frame and a shock absorber. It took two months to build the first prototype and friends and family thought he was crazy. But when they realized his self-styled construction could actually power their radios and charge their mobile phones, they were more appreciative. William has since added a second windmill, solar panels, bright lighting and a well. Climate change campaigners around the world, including Al Gore, and global business leaders have recognized his pioneering work, and William is well on the way to setting up his own windmill company to bring electricity and water to rural villages.

Chapter 17

THE END, THE BEGINNING, THE PERMANENT EDGE

And so we come to the end, or rather the beginning. Wiser people than me have said that it is not the destination that counts but the journey, and of course they are right. We cannot ever know the destination and I hope I have explained clearly enough that for all my talk of strategy, I am not pretending that I or you, or anyone, can really know the outcome of any endeavour in advance.

So this book has not been about promising outcomes, but rather about trying to help you to develop the tools to enable you to undertake your own journey more effectively. None of the tools are in themselves magic bullets, and there are no guarantees.

Well, actually, that's not quite right. There is one guarantee, which is simply that if you absorb the key points about building a 'brand' for yourself, then you will be better equipped for your journey than another person of equal talents and abilities who does not take a strategic, brand-building approach. In other words, the approaches in this book will give you an edge. How you use that edge is up to you.

The core concepts in this book were derived originally from my experience and observation of the world of business and branding for commerce. But don't let that fact throw you off the scent. In recent years the heads of charities and leaders of every kind of organization, even the governments of nations, have come to realize the power of branding in enabling them to communicate a distinctive and compelling narrative to the world.

Your edge will derive from you taking the same principles and applying them to your life's ambitions, in every sphere. Most individuals haven't yet caught on to the power of using the discipline of personal branding. And even a few years in the future, when many more people will be trying to create personal brands, most of them will be doing so on a relatively superficial level. The reason this book does not dwell on social media and other specific networking and communication techniques is because your edge will ultimately derive from focusing on much more profound and strategic aspects.

It's great to be involved in social media. It's great to network. Just as it is great to master the art of the firm handshake and to make confident and friendly eye contact. But these things are not your brand. Your brand, as you know well by now, is what you 'mean' to the world.

By now, if you have worked through the chapters and exercises in this book, you should have a much clearer idea of what you want to mean to the world, and a powerful set of story elements to help you communicate that meaning to your audiences. Please remember, as you move forwards, that You are one of your audiences, and that by communicating constantly with yourself you will draw strength and guidance.

I have emphasized throughout, however, that there is a profitable balance to be struck between being true to yourself and valuable to your audiences. I don't recommend self-indulgence, at least not if you are trying to build a personal brand, which must ultimately be an outwards-looking activity, not a self-indulgent one. The importance of this balance is, perhaps, the most important message of this book.

I think the second most important message is that your 'story' is your most powerful weapon. Without a story a CV is just a CV; facts are just facts; events are simply events; personal strengths and flaws are just those. We all have good and bad facts and events in our lives, and we all have more and less attractive aspects to our personalities. It can seem like chaos, but we can use the power of storytelling, which is such a profoundly important human tool, to give sense to the chaos. And by giving sense to our past by the creation of narrative, we can also create a narrative for our future.

In my experience it seems that many of us are unable to make positive and ambitious change in our lives simply because we can't see a narrative thread or thrust to our existence, or when we do see one we make the mistake of believing it is written by circumstances and not by our will. Remember my tree image? I would urge you to visualize that image and to contemplate it again. Its message is the heart of this book, because the branding process is not about the superficial elements of life, but about personal change and growth by taking control of your role in the world.

Finally, the third most important idea in the book, and the thing that I want to emphasize most of all to you in closing, is the idea of authenticity. There is nothing in the enterprise of developing a powerful, positive, highly distinctive, compelling and appealing personal brand that requires you to be inauthentic. You don't have to make things up. You don't have to be cleverer, or more talented, or more beautiful, or thinner, or better qualified, or richer, or better connected. You don't even have to exaggerate your appeal.

All you really have to do is be you: but with the insight (and this is where you will get your edge) that by examining your story, finding your strategy, paying heed to your audiences, and ultimately establishing the coherent set of meanings that we call a 'brand', you can be the same You but different. A reinvented You. A brand new You.

REAL-LIFE REINVENTORS ☻
Oprah Winfrey: chat show host

Oprah Winfrey's early life was humble. Born to a single teenage mother, she spent her first five years on her grandmother's farm while her mother looked for work. Aged six she was sent away to live with her mother and was repeatedly molested by male relatives and another visitor. The abuse lasted for years and was emotionally devastating. In her teens Oprah went to live with her father – a strict disciplinarian – and her life took a better turn. She flourished and became a prize-winning student, eventually winning a job with a local TV station as a reporter and anchor. Within a few years she was hosting her own chat show, which scored huge ratings and a worldwide reputation. In the 1990s her focus changed to emphasize spiritual values, healthy living and self-help. She also has extensive business interests, including magazines and cable channels. Forbes named Oprah as the first African-American woman to become a billionaire. She appears on every list of leading opinion makers and has had a profound influence on people around the world.

ACKNOWLEDGEMENTS

The biggest thanks of all go, as ever, to Sheila, for always keeping faith in our shared journey and for being a constant support and my dearest companion. It is inconceivable to me that I would ever achieve anything without you. Thanks also to Paul and to Alice: you both make me very proud. And to my Mum, of course, who in turn is disproportionately proud of me and to whom I owe so much.

Thank you to my agent, Diane Banks, and to Hay House for allowing this book to come to life. Thanks to everyone involved in our band, The Proposition, for giving me a vehicle to express the other side of my character, and for such a cool musical adventure.

Thanks to the many clients of my consultancy Brand Strategy Guru, who have allowed me to make a contribution to their brand stories, and to the team of outstanding professionals with whom I have been privileged to work.

Thank you also to the hundreds of customers around the world of Banjos Direct and Left Hand Bear, and to the small but dynamic team that has helped these businesses to take flight.

Thanks to the friends who have been so supportive and positive about my late-bloomer attempts to fulfil a lifetime's ambition to write professionally.

Finally, thanks to Kate Portman and Liz Hollis for researching many of the real-life reinvention stories that appear throughout this book.

ABOUT THE AUTHOR

Photographer: Claudia Gannon

Simon Middleton has always seen life as a great adventure and has successfully reinvented himself and his career several times.

He is the creator of the UK's leading specialist banjo retail brand, Banjos Direct, and he advises other entrepreneurs and organizations how to create outstanding brand stories.

Simon speaks at conferences worldwide about branding and personal change issues, and is a popular business and self-development author. His first book – *Build A Brand In 30 Days* (Capstone, 2010) – has become the definitive manual for small business owners, and his second – *What You Need To Know About Marketing* (Capstone, 2011) – is a boardroom guide to the big concepts of marketing.

Unusually for a businessman, Simon is also a performing musician. He is singer, guitarist and frontman of acoustic band The Proposition, whose debut album King Snake, Devil Shake was released in 2012 to critical acclaim.

As one of the UK's highest profile branding experts he appears frequently on BBC, CNN, Sky, Bloomberg and other TV channels, commenting on brand stories. He is confident that he is the only singing banjo shop owner ever to be interviewed by Jeremy Paxman.

Simon originally trained as a primary school teacher, then earned his spurs in PR before becoming a registered nurse for people with severe learning disabilities. He has also been a magazine editor, as well as the creative director of one advertising agency and the joint MD of another.

He lives in Norwich (which he claims is the finest city, in the finest county, in England). He has been married to Sheila, a singer and artist, since they were teenagers, and they have two grown-up children.

http://simonmiddleton.com